Celtic Worsh

Through the Year

Celtic Worship Through the Year

Prayers, readings and
creative activities for
ordinary days and saints' days

Compiled by
RAY SIMPSON

Hodder & Stoughton
LONDON SYDNEY AUCKLAND

First published in Great Britain 1997.

This edition 1998.

10 9 8 7 6 5 4 3

British Library Cataloguing in Publication Data.
A record for this book is available from the British Library.

ISBN 0 340 68667 7

Typeset by Kenneth Burnley in Irby, Wirral, Cheshire.
Printed and bound in Great Britain by
Mackays of Chatham PLC, Chatham, Kent

Hodder and Stoughton Ltd
A Division of Hodder Headline PLC
338 Euston Road
London NW1 3BH

I dedicate this book to George Carey,
Archbishop of Canterbury,
because of his willingness,
from the Chair of the Roman Augustine,
to take seriously the worship needs of the
emerging grass roots culture.

CONTENTS

Preface by Ian Bradley   viii
Introduction   xi
How to use this Worship Book   xiii

Worship Through the Week
Morning Worship for Sunday and the Easter Season   3
Morning Worship for Monday and the Trinity Season   8
Morning Worship for Tuesday and the Michaelmas Season   13
Morning Worship for Wednesday and the Advent Season   17
Morning Worship for Thursday and
     the Incarnation Season   21
Morning Worship for Friday and the Passion Season   25
Morning Worship for Saturday and the Creation Season   29
A Midday Prayer   32
An Alternative Midday Prayer   34
An Irenaeus Midday Prayer   36
Evening Worship for Sunday to Wednesday   39
Evening Worship for Thursday to Saturday   44
Friday Evening Prayer Around the Cross   49
Saturday Evening Vigil of Fire   53

Five Night Prayers, or Night Caps
General Theme   61
Brigid Theme   64
Resurrection Theme   66
Pentecost Theme   68
Michaelmas Theme   70

A Celtic Holy Communion 75

Some Special Celebrations
Evening Worship for the Winter Solstice 85
An Alternative Christmas 89
New Year 94
Easter Eve Vigil 97
Easter Sunrise Service 105
Ascension 109
Pentecost 113
Summer Earth Blessing 118
Harvests 124
Healing the Land – with a Whitby model 128
Prayer Walks – with a Glastonbury model 138

Praying with the Celtic Saints
Prayers, readings, biographies and places to visit
St Fursey – 16th January 145
St Brigid – 1st February 151
St David – 1st March 158
St Chad – 2nd March 163
St Patrick – 17th March 167
St Cuthbert – 20th March 174
St Brendan – 16th May 180
St Columba – 9th June 186
St Samson – 28th July 193
Glastonbury saints – 31st July 200
St Oswald – 5th August 204
St Ninian – 26th August 210
St Aidan – 31st August 217
Halloween and All Saints – 31st October/1st November 223
St Hilda – 17th November 229

An Everyday Prayer Guide Through the Celtic Year 235
Notes 249
Sources and Acknowledgments 250

Preface

The extraordinary revival of interest that has taken place over the last decade or so in the beliefs and practices of the first native Christian communities in the British Isles has brought many practical blessings in its wake. Perhaps the most significant is the refreshment and enrichment which it has given to worship in churches and among groups of many different denominational and theological persuasions.

Celtic Christianity is a unifying force. It brings us back to our common Christian ancestry and heritage and cuts through the numerous divisions and barriers that have been created by Christians over the last thousand years or so. It is also an enormously vital and creative force, full of transforming and transfiguring energy and with great potential, which we are only beginning to realise, to unclog the hardened arteries of our over-wordy and conceptualised ways of worshipping God and to release simpler, deeper and more meaningful wells of prayer and praise which have for too long been blocked up and disused. More directly, the Celtic Christian tradition, which has never died and continues to inform the spirituality and devotion of Christians in many of the so-called remoter parts of our islands, supplies a marvellous treasure trove of prayers, poems, blessings and hymns which are being used and adapted by many Christians today in both public worship and private devotion.

Worship was central to the life of the Christian communities that flourished in the British Isles between the sixth and tenth centuries AD. They went about their daily tasks conscious of

God's presence and blessing in even the most mundane aspects of life. They steeped themselves in the language and imagery of the Psalms and met regularly together to praise God, to express their deep penitence to Him for their failings and to ask for His protection in a dangerous and threatening world. I am struck by the way that these three over-arching themes of praise, penitence and protection shape the liturgies which are collected in this volume. I am also struck by the central role which they accord to the reading or singing of the Psalms, those greatest of all devotional works which express not just human praise of God but also the anger, questioning, despair and desolation which are also an authentic part of our condition and our offering and response to our Creator and Redeemer.

There are now a good number of books about Celtic Christianity. They include Ray Simpson's own excellent study *Exploring Celtic Spirituality*. What we have lacked until now is an easily accessible resource book of Celtic liturgies which can be used alike for public worship in church, small-group worship and individual devotion. In the time that I have been associated with the Community of Aidan and Hilda as an academic adviser and consultant I have been enormously impressed by both the quality and integrity of the liturgical material which it has produced, most of which is gathered together in this volume. I have also been impressed by the deep spirituality and broad-minded eirenicism of Ray Simpson, who has courageously followed the call to live alone on Lindisfarne following the way of the Celtic Saints.

No one is suggesting that the prayers which appear in the pages that follow were those actually said by Columba or Patrick. For a start, they would have prayed in Latin or old Irish and we have virtually no records of the forms of liturgy used in ancient Armagh or Iona. What one can say, however, is that the material presented in this volume, with its valuable and welcome use of modern and contemporary language, belongs to an authentic and distinctive Celtic Christian tradition. It has many of the hallmarks of that tradition as it has been passed down and developed over the last 1,500 years – a simplicity, freshness and directness of imagery, a rhythm and brevity which gives it an essentially poetic quality. It is shot through, too, with the themes that we know preoccupied Patrick, Columba and their contemporaries and followers – the presence of God in all things, the reality of His protective power and enfolding love, the blessings of creation, the closeness of the angels and the hosts of heaven and the sense of being ever surrounded by the great cloud of witnesses and the communion of saints.

This book provides an enormously rich resource for all who seek to sing a new song to God and to refresh our sometimes tired and stale ways of coming into His presence and speaking to Him. Ray Simpson has presented and structured it in both a helpful and a very sensitive way which should make it not just acceptable but positively enriching for churches and individuals of many different traditions and persuasions. I warmly commend *Celtic Worship Through the Year* in the prayerful hope that as we look towards a new millennium it will help to enliven our worship, deepen our devotion and, above all, draw us closer together in Christ.

Ian Bradley
Department of Church History
King's College
The University of Aberdeen

March 1997

Introduction

Culture is changing fast. Patterns of worship that reflect a distant church culture no longer connect. People are hungry for worship that reflects their heart-cries, yet which also has roots.

These patterns of worship have arisen out of a deep conviction that our worship needs to draw on our historic roots of Celtic Christianity, and also to be rooted in our contemporary world. They were written in the first place for use by members of the Community of Aidan and Hilda.[1] After being pilot tested and revised they are now offered to a wider public – to churches, to people in 'the alternative scene', and to individuals of many colours, temperaments and beliefs who make up our common home.

Celtic principles of worship are basically the same as those of universal Christianity, but some western liturgy has become wooden, wordy, overlaid; it has forgotten the Incarnation – God in everyday life. Celtic worship restores the balance: it relates God to every part of life, it re-kindles a vivid awareness of God's presence, it restores rhythm, it lights up heaven, and it invites us to worship 'with the five-stringed harp', that is, with all five senses.

In Celtic worship each chore becomes a liturgy. Confession is not a perfunctory statement, it is a heartfelt outpouring of sorrow. Blessings are no mere formularies, they are a consecration, an inclusion of the mundane within the sacred that confers grace and protection, a bringing forth of the potential in the thing blessed.

The need for such worship patterns is beginning to be recognised within the churches. The Anglican Church in New Zealand, for example, combines Maori with European prayer in its *A New Zealand Prayer Book* (Collins). The Church of Scotland's new *Book of Common Order* (St Andrew Press) includes a Celtic Order of Holy Communion. The Archbishop of Canterbury, Dr George Carey, has written that 'since the publication of the *Alternative Service Book 1980* our knowledge of the origin and purpose of daily common prayer in the early church has grown enormously. As a result, many people long for a return to a simple and more celebratory form of common prayer for our time.'[2] Worship patterns for today not only need to make room for reflection, they also need to be earthy, socially and ecologically aware, to provide for the use of spiritual gifts and creative arts.

And they need one thing more. Brother Roger of the Taizé Community has written: 'Since the sixteenth century words have gradually invaded the churches, to such an extent that the worship of the People of God risks being an intellectual exercise rather than radiant Communion'.[3] My prayer is that this worship book will help us to experience radiant communion.

A renaissance of such worship may give back a sense of direction to our lands.

Ray Simpson
Lindisfarne Retreat
Holy Island
Northumberland
TD15 2SD

How to use this Worship Book

This book is a resource for encouraging worship of God the Father, Son and Holy Spirit which is awesome, intimate and creative. An openness to ways of drawing on symbolism, Scripture and the Spirit will enrich and deepen the worship.

Please, therefore, do not see these patterns as rigid liturgies. Flexibility in the way they are used is to be welcomed and encouraged. The place of singing, open prayer, waiting on God, singing or praying in the Spirit, and the use of other material may be varied and developed according to local custom and circumstances. Greater use of traditional canticles may be preferred by some. The notes in the liturgies are only for guidance.

These patterns of worship draw on different traditions of spirituality. Where the theological emphasis does not sit comfortably with your own, please be free to modify the words, rather than reject the liturgy as inappropriate.

Use by individuals

These patterns of worship are suitable for use by individuals, with a few adaptations. For example, you may find it helps to omit the responses that are to be said by all.

Readers who believe that only a priest or minister should pronounce the forgiveness of sins may turn the absolution into a prayer; for example: 'May almighty God have mercy upon me and forgive me all my sins. . . .'

Use in formal church settings

In non-liturgical churches the leader may omit responses to be said by everyone, or may decide to say all, or most, of the words.

Use in informal or 'alternative' settings

In small groups it may seem good to involve as many people as possible in the worship, and a different person may be the reader for each item.

In 'alternative' worship the printed words may form only a small part of the whole, and the Creative Activities will take up the major part. During or after readings or talks there may be artwork, mime, dance, drama, or audiovisuals that illustrate the message. Before the prayers, interviews or discussion may draw out the concerns that are in the news. Long periods of contemporary music or drumming may be combined with silent prayer before candles or ikons, with rhythmic prayer breathing or movements, pictures, dance, or walks with inter-cession sticks, flags, and incense.

Selecting the Psalms and Bible readings of the day

If you already use a lectionary produced by a Christian church or network, we encourage you to continue to use this. The notes[4] on page 247 give details of these. If you do not, or these do not provide what you need, we suggest this:

Psalms: choose different key verses from Psalm 1 for the Morning, Midday and Evening Prayer today. Next time you use this worship book, do the same from Psalm 2, and so on.

Midday Prayer Bible readings: suggestions are included in the text.

Morning and evening readings: Start at the beginning of the Old Testament and read a paragraph or two each morning and evening (leaving out long lists or 'repeats'). Do the same with the New Testament. Keep a note of where you have got to.

Ways to read the Psalms

It is good to use varied ways, such as:

- One reader (at the end everyone may sing an Alleluia);
- One reader who asks everyone to repeat a key phrase (indicated by a raised hand, a pause, a nod or by a response leader);
- Two readers (perhaps male and female) who read alternate verses or stanzas;
- A leader and everyone else alternate verses;
- Chanting;
- A reader (or a group) dramatise the words;
- 'Monastic' intoning, used when everyone has a translation which has a colon in the middle of each verse at which everyone pauses. People in opposite rows read alternate verses.

Margin indications

The following margin indications are used:

- Leader – the leader of worship;
- Reader – the reader of scripture;
- Any – Anyone may lead with these words;
- All – all who are present.

Declaring forgiveness after confession

The manner of declaring forgiveness should follow the tradition, theology, and authority of the local worshipping community. If there is nobody suitable present, Scriptures such as 1 John 1:9 may be read as a reminder of the assurance of forgiveness.

The use of charismatic gifts

These are part of the ancient tradition of the church and some readers may wish to use these in any of the settings. A suitable time for singing in tongues is after a Thanksgiving. A suitable time for speaking or writing any prophetic message is after the time of silence. A suitable time to lay on hands for healing prayer, or to invite the Holy Spirit to come anew in a 'bathing time', is at the close of the prayer time or after the blessing, for those who wish to stay on.

Singing in the Spirit may take several forms such as repeated, instinctive singing of chants or jubilating, as was done at the enthronement of some of the popes.

What about saints?

According to the New Testament all Christians are called to be saints, which means holy people. So why have traditional churches selected only certain Christians to be known as saints? Because some Christians are more saintly than others, and we need to focus on a 'cloud of witnesses to God' (Hebrews 12:1) who inspire us to live as saints should. This book uses the term 'saints' for the sake of simplicity, but this does not question that every Christian has a direct access to God through Jesus.

Christians from high Anglican, Orthodox and Roman Catholic traditions believe that since Jesus gives us access to heaven, it is right and natural to talk with the saints, who are with Him. However, since some Christians prayed to saints because they feared to talk directly to God, other churches discourage this practice.

Celtic Christians were vividly aware of the whole company of heaven, and Columba taught us to 'make friends of the dead'; but they were clear that Jesus, who is always with us, alone makes this possible. In this book saints are only addressed through Jesus, so churches who address saints directly need to slightly adapt the words. (Angels are addressed directly in the Michaelmas Night Prayer, following the example of the Psalmist, e.g. Psalm 103:20.)

Use of these patterns of worship in churches whose worship is controlled by law

The worship material in this book is for use in and beyond all churches. In a few denominations, such as the Church of England, worship for all occasions envisaged in its canon law is regulated by that canon law. Nowadays, there are many occasions when members of the Church of England join Christians from other churches for occasions to which their canons do not apply. It is also possible to interweave these worship patterns into canonically prescribed liturgies.

Church of England clergy who wish to use these Patterns of Worship as a primary service in a parish church should note recent guidance from bishops. The Archbishop of Canterbury has observed that the intention of Cranmer's *Book of Common Prayer* was 'to help the church as a whole to pray together daily in a reflective and structured way' but that 'it only rather patchily achieved' this object.[5] He and other Church of England bishops have encouraged the use of simpler, contemporary patterns of prayer for use as the main non-eucharistic daily service in church, in order to enable church people to fulfil more adequately the intentions of canon law. The daily services in this book are written to this end.

With the Eucharist, there is a consensus that this should comply more to the letter of the canons. There are good reasons for this. The report of the world churches, *Baptism, Eucharist, Ministry*[6] concluded that whilst phraseology should vary according to local culture, certain elements of the Eucharist are too foundational to be optional. The Celtic Holy Communion on page 75 accords with its agreed list of essential elements. The Celtic Holy Communion is followed by notes for clergy in the Church of England which will enable them to celebrate the Celtic Eucharist according to canon law.

Music

Music has been omitted from this book for two reasons. Churches and groups differ widely in the style of music they use. Secondly, although there is much new material, from charismatic streams to the songs of the Iona Community, there remains a need for contemporary liturgical music that reflects Celtic renewal. The author would be glad to hear from people who have contributions to make.

Worship
Through the Week

ᗰorning ᗯorsᏂip

for Sunday and the Easter Season

 The Victory of Life over Death

Leader Christ is risen!
All He is risen indeed. Alleluia!

Leader Christ is risen from the wintry ground of death:
All Let all creation rise to greet its returning
Splendour.

Leader Christ is risen in victory over all powers of evil:
All Let all who know loss and destruction rise to greet
their returning Saviour.

Leader Christ is risen to renew the face of the earth:
All Let all who are parched rise to greet their
returning Spring.

Leader Christ is risen to form a new people of love:
All Let all who are abandoned rise to greet their
returning Spouse.

 There may be singing.

Springtime

To be said during Eastertide.

Leader Spring, with her colour, warmth, and scent: season
of budding, rebirth, intent.

All	Year by year He sends the spring: promise and pardon mingling.
Leader	While Christ eternal from the Cross: bounty bestows from utter loss.
All	The broken, cold, and stagnant earth: awakes with miracles of birth.
Leader	And spirits, broken, contrite, cold: are healed with blessings manifold.
All	At Eastertide the sap, the joy: runs barefoot like a little boy.
Leader	And hope grows warm with certainty: of miracles that we shall see.
All	Of harvest in the fields again: God's kingdom after death and pain.
Leader	Yes, death becomes a wondrous thing: mid Cross and crocus in the spring.
All	Beauty is free to walk abroad: and spread the glory of the Lord.
Leader	And still the sea obeys the will: of Him who whispered 'Peace, be still'.
All	That sea, its sounds and mystery: drew fishermen of Galilee.
Leader	For on the seashore Christ appeared: while Peter fished and others feared.
All	There Jesus lit the fire of faith: 'Christ is alive' and we are safe!
Leader	O, heaven is earth and earth is heaven: to know that Christ the King is risen;
All	To know the Easter tale is truc: that Jesus Christ makes all things new.

The great 'I Am'

This or the traditional Te Deum may be said outside Eastertide.

Leader Jesus said: I am the light of the world.
All Your light drives out the dark.

Leader I am the way, the truth, the life.
All Your way has brought true hope.

Leader I am the resurrection and the life.
All You broke the power of death.

Leader I am the bread of life.
All You feed and fill the hungry.

Leader I am the true vine.
All Your life becomes our life.

Leader I am the good shepherd.
All You guide and lead us on.

Leader Let us recollect the presence of the Risen Christ with us now.

Short silence.

Sorrow

Leader Lord Jesus, in the light of your risen presence, and in union with your first frail apostles, we say sorry:
All For not weighing your words and warnings;
For not staying with your shakings and shame;
For not believing your power and promise.
May we be finished with these ways for ever.

Leader The words of the Lord Jesus declare: your sins are forgiven, I give you my peace.
All We receive your peace and will walk in your risen life.

The Word of God

Reader *Psalm 30 or the Psalm of the day.*
Response for Psalm 30 (after verses 3, 5, 7, 10, 12):
All The Lord has raised me up.

There may be singing.

Reader Let us attend, the Word of God comes to us.
All Thanks be to God.
Reader Illumine our hearts, O Lord, implant in us a desire
for your truth; may all that is false within us flee.

Old Testament reading.

New Testament reading.

*Silence, teaching, sharing, a creed, or singing. The
following prayer may be expressed in movement and
colour.*

 Prayer

Leader Renew us, O Risen Christ:

In the midst of the staleness of routine, bring fresh
stirrings of life.
In the midst of creeping disillusion, bring
rekindled hope.
In the midst of numbing doubt, bring all-
conquering faith.
In the midst of shoddy expediency, bring
untarnished ideals.
In the midst of cold indifference, bring warm,
tender mercy.
In the midst of unseemly clamour, bring restored
serenity.

There may be free prayer, the Lord's Prayer, or everybody may act out this prayer followed by a time of music-making.

Leader   May Sunday be a day of resurrection; a day of refreshment for families and single people, for traders and communities. May our homes be places of hospitality and hope, that we may know your risen presence as we share lives and enjoy the company of others. May our churches worship in a way that brings honour to you, joy to the people, and healing to the land.

Blessing

Leader   Christ is risen!
All   He is risen indeed! Alleluia!

Leader   The God of life go with you.
The Risen Christ beside you.
The vibrant Spirit within you.
All   Amen!

Morning Worship
for Monday and the Trinity Season

 **Father, Son and Spirit.
God in Community**

Leader   In the name of the Three who are Love:
Father, Son and Holy Spirit.

Leader   The Three who are over my head:
All   The Three who are under my tread.

Leader   The Three who are over me here:
All   The Three who are over me there.

Leader   The Three who in heaven do dwell:
All   The Three in the great ocean swell.

Leader   Pervading Three, O be with me:
All   Pervading Three, O be with me.

Leader   Eternal God and Father,
You create us by your power
And redeem us by your love:
Guide and strengthen us by your Spirit,
That as we give ourselves in love and service to
one another and to you,
We may reflect your nature here on earth,
Through Jesus Christ our Lord.

 There may be singing.

Psalm

Psalm 113 (for Trinity) or key verses of the psalm of the day.

Sorrow

Leader The Father is always present.
   All Forgive us for not reflecting your faithfulness.

Leader The Son is always self-giving.
   All Forgive us for living for ourselves.

Leader The Spirit always leads us on.
   All Forgive us for holding back.

Leader Almighty God, who forgives all who truly repent, have mercy upon you, pardon and deliver you from all your sins, confirm and strengthen you in all goodness, and keep you in life eternal.
   All Amen.

 There may be singing.

 The Word of God

Reader Let us attend, the Word of God comes to us.
   All Thanks be to God.

Reader Illumine our hearts, O Lord, implant in us a desire for your truth; may all that is false within us flee.

Old Testament reading.

Exodus 34:1–10 (for Trinity) or key verses of the reading for the day.

Protection

Leader For my shield this day I call:
Almighty power, the Holy Trinity.

All Faith in the Three, trust in the One:
Creating all through love.

Leader In faith I trust in the Father of all:
He is my refuge, a very strong wall.

All For my shield this day I call:
Christ's power in His coming.
Christ's power in His dying.
Christ's power in His rising.

Leader For my shield this day I call:
The mighty Spirit who breathes through all.

All Faith in the Three, trust in the One,
Making all through love.

Reader *New Testament reading.*

Mark 1:1–11 (for Trinity) or the reading of the day.

Silence, teaching, creative activity, or singing.

Creative Activity

Read through the following prayers. Now walk around the streets and make a list of everything you see which reflects the Trinity. Prepare prayers, role play or pictures that reflect what you have observed.

Prayers

Any of these, or other prayers may be said:

Leader Lord, we give you thanks for the little trinities that reflect your nature to us:
For the tender kiss, the friendly hug.
For the man and wife who make love and conceive.
For the babe who sucks its mother's breasts.

For the child playing with its parents.
For the fellowship of the air waves, of sport, music
and dance.
For the sun that is fire, light and warmth.
For the water that is liquid, steam and ice.

May the love of the Three give birth to a new
community.
May the friendship of the Three give birth to a new
humanity.
May the life of the Three give birth to a new
creativity.
May the togetherness of the Three give birth to a
new unity.
May the glory of the Three give birth to a new
society.

Trinity Triads

Leader   Power of all powers
All   We worship you.
Leader   Light of all lights
All   We worship you.
Leader   Life of all lives
All   We worship you.

Leader   Source of all life
All   We turn to you.
Leader   Saviour of all life
All   We turn to you.
Leader   Sustainer of all life
All   We turn to you.

Leader   Ground of all being
All   We rest in you.
Leader   Salt of all being
All   We rest in you.
Leader   Unity of all being
All   We rest in you.

Leader	Maker of all creatures
All	We honour you.
Leader	Friend of all creatures
All	We honour you.
Leader	Force of all creatures
All	We honour you.

Leader	Love before time
All	We adore you.
Leader	Love in dark time
All	We adore you.
Leader	Love in present time
All	We adore you.

*There may be free prayer, contributions from those
doing the creative activities, or singing.*

Blessing

Leader	Into the Sacred Three I immerse you.
	Into their power and peace I place you.
	May their breath be yours to live.
	May their love be yours to give.

Morning Worship

for Tuesday and the Michaelmas Season

 Good and evil in dark days

Leader   ✠ In the name of the God of angels,
In the name of the Saviour from ill,
In the name of the Spirit of all truth,
In the name of the Three we are still.

All   Amen.

Leader   At creation the angels sang in delight,

All   The world is vibrant with your messengers of joy.

Leader   At the birth of your Son they proclaimed your praise,

All   You are enthroned on your servants' praise.

Leader   As day follows night they follow your will,

All   To chase away dark and all shadow of sin.

The Greatness of Heaven

Leader   In the midst of dark powers,

All   We magnify the greatness of heaven.

Leader   In the midst of foul deeds,

All   We magnify the greatness of heaven.

Leader   In the midst of fearful thoughts,

All   We magnify the greatness of heaven.

Leader   In the midst of a blighted land,

All   We magnify the greatness of heaven.

Leader	In our time of need,
All	We magnify the greatness of heaven.

Leader	We praise you, Lord of heaven and earth,
All	Glorious God, we proclaim your worth.

 Psalm

Psalm 43 or key verses of the Psalm of the day are read.

Confession

Leader	The angels delight to do your will alone;
All	Forgive us for denying and defying your will.

Leader	Lord, have mercy.
All	Lord, have mercy.

Leader	The angels move freely unchecked by sin;
All	Forgive us for the restrictions caused by our sin.

Leader	Christ, have mercy.
All	Christ, have mercy.

Leader	The angels support the children of God;
All	Forgive us for discouraging the givers of love.

Leader	Lord, have mercy.
All	Lord, have mercy.

 Singing

 The Word of God

Reader	Let us attend, the sharp double-edged sword of the Word of God comes to us.
All	Thanks be to God.

Reader	Illumine our hearts, O Lord, implant in us a desire for your truth; may all that is false within us flee.

Old Testament reading.

This may be followed by a sung Alleluia.

New Testament reading.

There may be silent meditation, teaching, sharing or singing.

 Prayer

These or other prayers may be said:

Leader   Lord, may Michael, head of the angels, shield us with the power of his sword, and spread his wings over our homes and schools. Bring us help from heaven above. Be with us in the journeys and twistings of life. Guide us along the path of truth and away from any path of evil. Take from us all that harms.

Leader   Have mercy on little ones abused, may tender angels draw them to your presence.
Have mercy on those in black trial, may healing angels lift them into your presence.
Have mercy on souls at death's door, may holy angels escort them to your presence.
Have mercy on we who remain, may smiling angels radiate to us your presence.

Leader   In the name of the living God and His heavenly army, we stand against the rulers, authorities and powers of evil, seen and unseen.
Lord, deliver us from the powers of evil that have entrenched themselves in the structures of our society.

Deliver us from:
racial and religious prejudice;
exploitation and greed;
abortion and euthanasia;
sexual immorality and pornography;
family breakdown and isolation;
violence and crime;
witchcraft and the occult.

Any Lord, deliver us from . . . (*evils may be named*).

Leader Deliver us from every kind of evil and lead us not
into temptation.

All For yours is the kingdom, the power and the glory,
for ever and ever. Amen.

Blessing

Leader The shield of Christ be over you,
The shield of Michael militant safeguard you.
The shield of God's grace go with you,
To guard you from your back,
To preserve you from your front,
From the crown of your head to the soles of your
feet,
So that an island shall you be in the sea,
A hill shall you be on the land,
A well shall you be in the desert,
A light shall you be in the dark.

All Amen.

ᏝᏆᎾᏒᏁᎥᏁᏟ ᏔᎾᏒᏚᏂᎥᏢ

ᚠᎾᏒ ᏔᎬᏗᏁᎬᏚᏗᎧᏼ and ᏠᏂᎬ ᎯᏇᏴᎬᏁᏠ ᏚᎬᏗᏚᎾᏁ

 ### Preparing for the God of Destiny to come

Introduction

On special occasions this may be preceded by a candle-lit vigil of silence or drum-beats that build up a sense of anticipation.

Leader In the wasteland may the Glory shine.
In the land of the lost may the King make His home.

Let Us Wake

Leader Let us wake to Christ's summons, urgent in our midst:
All He comes to bring judgment nearer than we know.

Leader Let us wake to the truth that His power alone will last:
All The worlds that scorn Him will vanish like a dream.

Leader Let us wake to the truth that His glory can be seen:
All In all the deeds that sweeten, in all the thoughts that heal.

Leader	Let us wake to the truth that His reign is yet to come.
All	That routs out the world of evil; that fulfils the world of good.

 Psalm

Reader *Psalm 50:1–15 or key verses of the Psalm of the day are read.*

Sorrow

Leader	Lord, poets and parents-in-God picture and pattern your ways;
All	Forgive us for following idols and illusions.

A moment of silence.

Leader	Lord, prophets shine like candles in the night;
All	Forgive us for staying in the dark.

A moment of silence.

Leader	Lord, preachers like John the Baptist clear the way for you;
All	Forgive us for blocking your way.

A moment of silence.

Leader	Lord, the Virgin Mary offered her all as the bearer of your Life;
All	Forgive us for holding ourselves back.

There may be silence or words of forgiveness.

 **The Word of God**

Reader	Let us attend, the Word of God comes to us.
All	Thanks be to God.

Reader	Illumine our hearts, O Lord, implant in us a desire for your truth; may all that is false within us flee.

Old Testament reading.

Reader   Hear the Word of God from the Old Testament
                 in . . .

                 (at close):

Reader   This is the Word of the Lord.
   All   Thanks be to God.

Transforming the World

Leader   The earth is becoming a wasteland:
   All   Breath of the Most High, come and renew it.

Leader   Humanity is becoming a battleground:
   All   Child of Peace, come and unite it.

Leader   The world is becoming a playground:
   All   Key of Destiny, open doors to our true path.

Leader   The world is becoming a no-man's land:
   All   God-with-us, come and make your home here.

Leader   The planet is becoming a graveyard:
   All   Spring of God, come with buds of life.

New Testament reading.

Reader   Let us attend; Christ the living Word comes to us.
                 Hear the Word of Christ in . . .

                 The reading.

Reader   This is the Word of Christ.
   All   Praise to the coming King.

Leader   Calm us to wait for the gift of Christ;
                 Cleanse us to prepare the way for Christ;
                 Teach us to contemplate the wonder of Christ;
                 Touch us to know the presence of Christ;
                 Anoint us to bear the life of Christ.

Silent meditation may be followed by teaching, music, sharing or singing.

 Prayers

Words in brackets may be followed by free prayer or may be omitted.

Leader   Wisdom, Breath of the Most High, permeating and restoring creation, come and make us friends of God.
(Especially we pray for . . .)
Come, Lord Jesus, come.

All   Come, Lord Jesus, come.

Leader   Chief of God's people of old, you revealed yourself to Moses in the burning bush, and gave him laws to guide your people, come and dispel our confusion.
(Especially we pray for . . .)
Come, Lord Jesus, come.

All   Come, Lord Jesus, come.

Leader   King David's descendant, you are the key that opens the door to the destiny of each nation; come and release all that is good and creative in our people.
(Especially we pray for . . .)
Come, Lord Jesus, come.

All   Come, Lord Jesus, come.

The Lord's Prayer and free prayer may follow.

Blessing

Leader   The King of life appear to you;
The Son of life shed light on you;
The Spirit of life flow into you;
The Holy Three come near to you.

All   Amen.

Morning Worship

for Thursday and the Incarnation Season

 God in human form present in our world

Leader   Mary, chosen gateway, through her there came to earth,
The Bridge of Life to aid us, to give us eternal worth.

All   Glory to the Most High God who has come to live among us.

There may be singing.

Leader   Let us remember the glorious birth:
All   Glory to God in the highest.

Leader   God in His majesty came down to earth:
All   Glory to God in the highest.

Leader   To Mary the Virgin came the Spirit of life:
All   Glory to God in the highest.

Leader   She conceived and gave birth to Jesus the Christ:
All   Glory to God in the highest.

Leader   Now is born to us the root of our joy,
And the night stars gleam over mountains high.

All   Glow to Him wood and tree;
Glow to Him mount and sea;
Glow to Him land and plain;
Now His foot has come to earth.

There may be meditations or songs to Jesus.

Sorrow

Leader   Dear Son of God, change my heart.
You took flesh to redeem me; forgive my hardness;
Dear Son of Mary, change my heart.

All   Dear Son of God, take our hearts.
With sacrificial love you came for us;
Forgive our selfishness;
Dear Son of Mary, take our hearts.

There may be silence, spontaneous words of confession or words of forgiveness.

The Word of God

Reader   *Psalm 8 or key verses of the Psalm of the day.*

This may be followed by singing of Alleluias.

Reader   Let us attend, the Word of God comes to us.
All   Thanks be to God.

Reader   Illumine our hearts, O Lord, implant in us a desire for your truth; may all that is false within us flee.

Old Testament reading.

The Soles of His Feet

All   The soles of His feet have reached the earth,
The soles of the Son of Glory.
All the world gives homage to Him;

The sun on the housetops shines for Him;
The voice of the winds with the sounds of the streets
Announce to us that Christ is born.
God the Lord has opened a door;
The Door of Hope, the Door of Joy,
Golden Sun of earth and sky
All hail! Let there be joy!

Reader   Let us attend. Hear the Word of Christ in . . .

New Testament reading.

Silent meditation, teaching, sharing, music or singing.

 Prayers

Leader   Child of Glory, Child of Mary, born in the stable,
King of all; you came to our wasteland, in our
place suffered.

All   We greet you our Saviour, Brother and Lord.

Leader   Your birth binds heaven and earth together;
Bind us together in the kinship of one family
throughout the world.

All   May we be one with creation and one with all
peoples.

Leader   Your birth made possible the holy family.
All   Make families whole and holy today.

Leader   Babe of heaven, defenceless Love:
You had to travel far from your home.

All   Strengthen us as we make our pilgrimage of trust
on earth.

Leader   King of glory, you accepted such humbling.
All   Give us a serving spirit in all we do.

Leader   Your birth shows us the simplicity of the Father's
love, the wonder of being human.

All   Help us to live fully human lives for you.

Leader	Child of Glory, Child of Mary, you come with justice and peace. You come amongst the poor. Let us pray for these . . .
Any	. . .

There may be silence, singing or the Lord's Prayer.

Blessing

Leader	May the eternal Glory shine upon you; May the Son of Mary stay beside you; May the life-giving Spirit overshadow you; May the eternal Three be always with you.
All	Amen.

Morning Worship
for Friday and the Passion Season

 Appraisal in the light of Christ

Leader ✠ In the name of the searching Father;
In the name of the servant Son;
In the name of the purging Spirit;
In Love's name, the Three-in-One.

All Amen.

Leader On this day (or at this time) of the Saviour's passion, let us be one with Him in His wounds.

Leader We seek to tread in the steps of Christ;
All In the steps of Christ our Champion and King.

Leader He has shown us the way when strong, when weak;
All He is our Master in everything.

 Psalm

Reader *Read Psalm 22:1–19 or key verses of the Psalm of the day.*

Lamentation

After each lament there is a pause; examples may be given in silence or aloud.

Leader May I weep for pride and loose talk . . .
May I weep for the blame heaped on others . . .
May I weep for things I clutch at . . .

All	Strip from me, O God: Pretence and divided loyalties; Grudges and compulsive habits; Lustful alighting places; Unloving relationships; Self-sufficient attitudes.
Leader	May we weep for our hollow society . . . May we weep for neglect and brutality . . . May we weep for blighted lives . . .
All	May holy Jesus pardon us for these sins, Free us from these evils, And power us into new ways.

'Lord have mercy' or similar words may be said or sung several times.

The Word of God

Reader	Let us attend, the Word of God comes to us.
All	Thanks be to God.
Reader	Illumine our hearts, O Lord, implant in us a desire for your truth; may all that is false within us flee.

Old Testament reading.

Christ in Trials

Leader	Lord, you were born in an outhouse, an outsider:
All	Help us to sense you in our birth.
Leader	You were thirty years at the carpenter's bench:
All	Help us to find you in our work.
Leader	You were driven to the sands by the searching Spirit:
All	Strip from us what is not of you.
Leader	You were alone, without comfort or food:
All	Help us to rely on you alone.

Leader	You were tested by the evil one, you clung to no falsehood:
All	Break in us the hold of power and pride.
Leader	You knew deep tears and weakness:
All	Help us to be vulnerable for you.
Leader	You followed to the end the way of the Cross:
All	Help us to be faithful to you in all our ways.
Reader	*New Testament reading.*

On special occasions 'Christ in Trials' may be expressed visually.

There may be silent meditation, teaching, sharing or singing. The leader may invite free prayer after each of the following petitions.

Prayer

Leader   Christ of the scars, into your hands we place the broken, the wounded, the hungry and the homeless . . .

Christ of the scars, into your hands we place those who have been bereaved or betrayed; those who have suffered loss of health or esteem, family or friends, employment or home . . .

Christ of the scars, into your hands we place unwanted babies, children abused, neighbours defamed, lovers spurned, spouses deserted . . .

Christ of the scars, into your hands we place those who are victims of violence or vandalism, false accusation or sharp practice . . .

The Lord's Prayer, free prayer or a time of silent waiting may follow.

Leader Father, in the life of Jesus you have shown us the way.

All Give us His spirit of self-discipline; lead us more deeply into the way of the cross.

Leader Before His hands were stretched out on the cross, they were stretched out in love to children, women, and men.

All May your way of the Cross be our way, that we, too, may stretch out our hands in love to all.

The grace of our Lord Jesus Christ, the love of God, and the fellowship of the Holy Spirit be with us all, evermore. Amen.

ODorning Worship

for Saturday and the Creation Season

 Creation Cries Glory to God

Leader ✚ In the name of the creating Father,
In the name of the life-saving Son,
In the name of the resourcing Spirit,
In the name of the Three-in-One.
All Amen.

Leader Bless the Lord, O my soul:
All And forget not all His benefits.

Leader Bless Him for His creation:
All Which is alive with His glory.

Leader God nods and beckons to us:
All Through every stone and star.

 Psalm

Reader *Read Psalm 19:1–6 or key verses from the Psalm of the day.*

The Glory of Creation

Each sentence is followed by this response (R):

All We give you thanks, O Lord.

Leader	For earth and sea and sky in the harmony of colour. (R)
Leader	For the air of the eternal seeping through the physical. (R)
Leader	For the everlasting glory dipping into time. (R)
Leader	For nature resplendent, growing beasts, mergent crops, singing birds, the energies of the city. (R)
Leader	For the Person you sent to restore us when we fell away from the goodness of your creation. (R)
Leader	For harmony restored through His Spirit moving upon the turbulent waters of our lives. (R)
Leader	For the honour you give us of lives flowing in the rhythm of your tides. (R)
Leader	For setting each of us, like the stars upon their courses, within the orbit of your love. (R)

There may be singing.

The Word of God

Reader	Let us attend, the Word of God comes to us.
All	Thanks be to God.
Reader	Illumine our hearts, O Lord, implant in us a desire for your truth, may all that is false within us flee.

Old Testament reading.

All	I believe, O God of all gods,
	That you are the eternal Creator of life.
	I believe, O God of all gods,
	That you are the eternal Father of love.
	I believe, O Lord and God of the peoples,
	That you are the Creator of the high heavens.
	I believe, O Lord and God of the peoples,
	That you created my soul and set its warp.

Reader   *New Testament reading.*

There may be teaching, silent listening followed by sharing anything God has spoken or by confession, singing or the Lord's Prayer.

Prayers

Leader   We offer to you all we are, all we have, all we do, and all whom we shall meet this day, that you will be given the glory.

We offer to you our homes, our work, our schools. Fill them with simplicity, peace and love; may all be done as unto you.

We offer to you the coal and oil, the seas and soil, the air and animals; may we steward your creation to your glory and for the benefit of future generations.

We offer to you places and people on our hearts, and we name them now.

Any   *(places and people may be named)* . . .

All   Father, bless to me my body,
Father, bless to me my soul,
Father, bless to me all creatures,
Father, bless to me my goal.

Leader   You, O Lord, are the source of our life:
All   Fill us with your light and love.

Leader   Let us see your mighty deeds:
All   And walk in the hope of your kingdom.

Leader   Be with us all through this day:
All   Father, Son and Holy Spirit.

A Midday Prayer

Leader   In the name of the creating Father,
In the name of the workaday Son,
In the name of the renewing Spirit,
In the name of the Three-in-One.

There may be singing.

 A Psalm

*Read this verse from Psalm 127:1, 2. If there is time,
you could sing something before, and meditate after
reading it. Tomorrow, choose a verse from the next
Psalm, and so on each day.*

Reader   If the Lord does not build the house, the work of
the builders is useless. If the Lord does not build
the city, it is useless for sentries to stand guard. It is
useless to work so hard for a living, getting up
early and going to bed late. For the Lord provides
for those he loves.

 A Prayer

As the press of work pauses at noon,
May God's rest be upon us.
As the sun rides high at noon,
May the Sun of Righteousness shine upon us.
As the rain refreshes the stained, stale streets,
May the Spirit bring rain upon our dry ground.

A Bible verse

*Read and meditate on this verse from Ephesians
6:6, 7. Tomorrow begin to read Matthew chapters
5 to 7 and read one or two verses each day.*

Reader Obey those over you sincerely, with a proper sense
of respect and responsibility, as service offered to
Christ Himself. You may be sure that God will
reward a person for good work.

Prayers

The Lord's Prayer may be said.

Leader Lead me from death to life,
From falsehood to truth.
Lead me from despair to hope,
From fear to trust.
Lead me from hate to love,
From war to peace.
Deep peace of the Son of peace,
Fill our hearts, our workplace, our world.
Bless us now Lord, in the middle of the day;
Be with us and all who are dear to us
And be in the eye of each person we shall meet.
Keep us in the beautiful attitudes,
Joyful, simple and gentle.

Leader May the eye of the great God of glory,
The eye of the Virgin's Son,
The eye of the gentle Spirit,
Look after us in every moment;
And pour upon us mildly and generously hour by
hour.

An Alternative Midday Prayer

I bow before your Presence,
You who are common to us all.

*Rhythmic breathing of the name 'Jesus' . . . As you
breathe out the last syllable 'us', let tensions, hurts or
failures flow out like an ebbing tide. As you breathe in
the first syllable 'Je', desire to be filled with the fullness
and goodness of God.*

Fill me with the Deep Wisdom.
Fill me with the Great Compassion.
Fill me with the Serene Peace. *(Pause)*

Let forgiveness flow.
Let love come forth.
Let energy return. *(Pause)*

Deep peace of the quiet earth.
Deep peace of the flowing air.
Deep peace of the floating spheres.
Deep peace of the Son of peace.

Silent communion with the Source of all.

Read a Bible verse.

Kindle in us the fire of love.
Bring us alive.
Give warmth to our work.

Dear Jesus, at this hour you hung on the Cross, stretching out your arms in love to all. May all the peoples of the world be drawn to your love, especially the people I shall work with next.

Realising that we are all nourished from the same source, may we so live that others are not deprived of food or friends, of shelter or smiles, of pure air or good earth, or of the desire to live fully human lives.

Take time to visualise this prayer:

Your kingdom come.
Your will be done.
On earth as it is in heaven.

The eternal Creator keep us.
The beloved Companion beside us.
The Spirit's smile upon us.

An Irenaeus
Midday Prayer

 Glory in the work

Irenaeus, the early church leader in Celtic Gaul, taught that 'the glory of God is seen in a human life fully lived'.

Leader   Glory to God above.
Glory to Christ beside.
Glory to the Spirit within.

Lord come and put a glory in my work today.
Come and put a shine on the noontime fray.
May the Glory come now from the heavens high.
The Glory come to me; the Glory come nigh.

 Psalm

Reader   *Read key verses from Psalm 8 (below) or from the Psalm following yesterday's.*

O Lord, our Lord, your majesty is seen in all the world.
What is a human being that you care for her so much?
You made him second only to yourself.
You crowned her with glory and honour.
O Lord, our Lord, your majesty is seen in all the world.

Leader   May the glory of God be seen in work that is done from the heart.

May the glory of God be seen in commerce that
meets true needs.
May the glory of God be seen in communication
that ennobles the spirit.
May the glory of God be seen in clean and honest
living.
May the glory of God be seen in the delights of
sexual union.
May the glory of God be seen in the athlete who
goes all out.
May the glory of God be seen in beauty of art and
form.
May the glory of God be seen in architecture that
inspires.
May the glory of God be seen in the pursuit of true
learning.

Silence

May the glory of God be seen in the stature of
waiting.
May the glory of God be seen in the grace of
unknowing.
May the glory of God be seen in the dignity of
humbling.

Reader   We reflect like mirrors the glory of the Lord. The
Lord, who is the Spirit, transforms us in ever-
increasing glory into God's image. *(2 Corinthians
3:18)*

There are varieties of work, but the same Spirit
gives work for everyone to do. Each person is given
a gift by God's Spirit to use for the common good.

*1 Corinthians 12:4, 5 or other key verses from this or
the next chapter may be read.*

Leader   The glory of God in my working.
              The glory of God in my speaking.
              The glory of God in my eating.
              The glory of God in my resting.
              The glory of God in my thinking.
              The glory of God in my looking.
              The glory of God in my listening.
              The glory of God in my travelling.
              The glory of God in my crying.
              The glory of God in my loving.
              The glory of God in the present moment.

Arms of the glorious Three be around those we shall work with, and may the glorious Three pour lovingly and generously upon us, and upon all who are with us, hour by hour.

Evening Worship
for Sunday to Wednesday

 Proclaiming the Light

Leader   *Sunday:*
Spirit of the Risen Christ,
As the lamps light up the evening,
Shine into our hearts and kindle in us the fire of
your love.

Monday:
Holy Three, draw near to us with your encircling
light;
Kindle in us the fire of your love.

Tuesday:
Send us, O Lord, the light of your truth;
Dispel the darkness of sin and ignorance.

Wednesday:
Prepare the way of the Lord,
Who comes to light up our darkness.

Candles may be lit.

These words may be said or sung:

Leader   The light of Christ has come into the world.
   All   The light of Christ has come into the world.

The following or a hymn may be sung or said:

   All   Light of the world, in grace and beauty,
Mirror of God's eternal face,
Transparent flame of love's free duty,

You bring salvation to our race.
Now, as we see the lights of evening,
We raise our voice in hymns of praise.
Worthy are you of endless blessing,
Sun of our night, lamp of our days.

 Psalm

Reader *Key verses from the Psalm of the day are read.*
This may be followed by a brief silence.

Leader We offer to you, Lord, the troubles of this day;
We lay down our burdens at your feet.
Forgive us our sins, give us your peace,
And help us to receive your Word.

All In the name of Christ. Amen.

 The Word of God

There may be a reading from the Old Testament.

Reader Let us attend. Hear the Word of God in . . .

(at close):

Reader This is the Word of the Lord.
All Thanks be to God.

There may be a reading from the New Testament.

There may be teaching, silent reflection, confession or a creed.

 Giving of Thanks

There may be singing.

Leader We give you thanks, O Lord, that you are always
present, in all things, each day and each night.
We give you thanks for your gifts of creation, life
and friendship. We give you thanks for the
particular blessings of this day . . .

There may be a brief pause, the naming of blessings, singing in tongues or a song.

Intercessions

Some traditions may wish to use a sung response (R) or incense:

Leader   Into your hands, O Lord, we place our families, our neighbours, our brothers and sisters in Christ, and all whom we have met today . . . enfold them in your will. (R)

Leader   Into your hands, O Lord, we place all who are victims of prejudice, oppression or neglect; the frail, the unwanted . . . May everyone be cherished from conception to the grave. (R)

Leader   Into your hands, O Lord, we place all who are restless, sick, or prey to the powers of evil . . . keep guard over them. (R)

Leader   Into your hands, O Lord, we place the concerns of this day . . . *(the prayer theme for the day).*

Sunday:

Risen Christ –
May this day bring refreshment to the earth . . . traders . . . families . . . communities . . .
May unity grow in the Body of Christ.
May our churches bring honour to you in their worship, and faith and healing to the people . . .
Bring renewal to the ordained ministry . . . to religious communities . . . and raise up new vocations, new communities, which meet the need of our times.

Monday:

Carpenter Christ –
We offer you the daily work of the world . . .
industry, commerce, transport, technology . . .
those in dangerous jobs . . . the workless and the
underpaid . . . those engaged in research and
development . . . those seeking to understand
the laws behind politics, economics and
government . . .
May the wealth and work of the world be
available to all and for the exploitation of none . . .
May employers, shareholders and employees work
together like fingers on a hand . . .
May those who administer justice have truth and
integrity . . .
May all our work be done as unto you.

Tuesday:

Teaching Christ –
May education find its inspiration as staff,
students and sponsors are taught by you . . .
We offer to you pre-school children . . . primary
schools . . . secondary schools . . . colleges . . .
universities . . . informal learning networks . . .
We offer to you scientists, inventors, space
researchers . . . those teaching new skills to people
with special needs and in prisons . . . overseas
students . . . young people who feel alienated . . .
youth movements . . .
We pray for homes to be wellsprings of wisdom . . .
for women to welcome the divine artistry and
sacrifice of motherhood . . . for fathers to be priests
to their families . . .

Wednesday:

Healing Christ –
Bring healing to the land . . .
We offer to you the fields and forests, the farms
and fisheries . . . may we steward your creation to
your glory and for the benefit of future
generations.
We offer to you the Health Services . . . the Armed
Services . . . homes for orphans, refugees, the
elderly . . . hospices . . .
We pray for healing of families . . .
We pray for the healing ministries of the church . . .

Any *(Free prayer)*

Leader Lord Jesus Christ, Light of the world,
By your Cross you have overcome all darkness
that oppresses.
Come and shine on us here in . . .
That we may grow and live together in your love
Which makes us one with all humanity.

All The grace of our Lord Jesus Christ, the love of God,
and the fellowship of the Holy Spirit, be with us all
evermore. Amen.

*It is possible to use either form of Evening Worship on
any day, using the introductory words and the
intercessions for the day.*

*The Daily Intercessions may also be used by people
who simply want to pray in their own way each day,
but with a sense that they are sharing a rhythm and
focus for prayer that have grown out of the experience
of God's people in other times and places.*

Evening Worship
for Thursday to Saturday

 Renewing the Peace

Note that Prayer Around the Cross and the Vigil of Fire may replace Evening Worship on Fridays and Saturdays, but the Intercessions should be included.

Leader   *Thursday:*
Holy, holy, holy is the eternal Flame undying,
Burning here amongst us in sacrificial love.

Friday:
Open our eyes to your presence, open our ears to your call;
Open our hearts to your mercies; tonight be our
All in all.

Saturday:
May we welcome the light in all creation
Which is streaming from the Sun of suns.

Candles or spotlights may be lit.

We give you thanks that you led our forebears in the Faith by a pillar of cloud by day and a pillar of fire by night; we give you thanks, kindly Light, that the torch of faith was brought to this land, and that you ever lead your people on. Light up

our dark hearts, O God, by the light of your Christ;
may His Word illumine our way, for you pour
forth your kindness on all your creation, Father,
Saviour, and radiant Spirit.

All   May the Light of lights come to my dark heart;
May the Spirit's wisdom come to me from my
Saviour.
Be the peace of the Spirit mine this night,
Be the peace of the Son mine this night,
Be the peace of the Father mine this night,
The peace of all peace be mine this night,
Each morning and evening of my life.

There may be singing.

Psalm

Reader   *Key verses from the Psalm of the day are read followed
by a brief silence.*

Leader   We offer to you, Lord, the troubles of this day;
We lay down our burdens at your feet.
Forgive us our sins, give us your peace,
And help us to receive your Word.

All   In the name of Christ. Amen.

The Word of God

There may be a reading from the Old Testament.

Leader   Lord, you are my island, in your bosom I rest.
All   You are the calm of the sea, in that peace I stay.

Leader   You are the deep waves of the shining ocean,
All   With their eternal sound I sing.

Leader   You are the song of the birds, in that tune is my joy,
All   You are the smooth white strand of the shore, in
you is no gloom.

Leader You are the breaking of the waves on the rock,
your praise is echoed in the swell.

All You are the Lord of my life; in you I live.

Silence or informal thanksgiving.

Reader *A reading from the New Testament.*

Teaching or silent reflection on the Word; occasionally this may lead to confession.

There may be singing.

Intercessions

Leader *Thursday:*

Christ of the Sacrament –
We thank you that in the Eucharist we have a vision of your Presence transforming all creation, enabling human life to be lived to the full . . .
We pray for the re-kindling of a Christian imagination and of the vision of God on earth.
We offer to you the press and TV, artists and writers, musicians and worship leaders, prophets and poets, promoters and publishers, that they may glimpse this vision, and reflect it to the world.

Friday:

Christ of the scars –
May the benefits of your passion flow into the broken and the wounded, the lonely and the unwanted, the hungry and the homeless, the addicted and the aimless, the despairing and the dying . . .
May they flow into the places of darkness, racial conflict, division and death in our world . . .
We forgive our enemies and bless them . . .

May those who do not know you come to know
your presence alongside them . . .

Saturday:

Christ of the lakeside –
We offer you the world of leisure and sport, trade
and travel . . .
We pray for fitness of mind, body and spirit . . .
for the finding and following of true callings . . .
for freedom from debt . . . for hospitable homes . . .
for safe streets . . .
We pray for generous giving to God's work . . .
that we may become a generous society . . .
We pray that God's people may pray and prepare
worthily to celebrate your resurrection . . .

The Circling Prayer

Leader   Circle us, Lord –
Keep darkness out, keep light within.
Keep fear without, keep peace within.
Keep hatred out, keep love within.

The leader may invite anyone to add to these.

Any   Circle us, Lord –
Keep . . . out, keep . . . within.

*The leader may invite anyone to pray the circling
prayer for groups or places.*

Leader   Circle . . . , Lord –
Keep . . . without, keep . . . within.

Any   Circle . . . , Lord –
Keep . . . without, keep . . . within.

There may be singing.

Leader   Lighten our darkness, Lord, we pray; and in your great mercy defend us from all dangers and perils of this night; for the love of your only Son, our Saviour, Jesus Christ.

Friday Evening Prayer Around the Cross

 People gather in silence to kneel or sit around a cross or crucifix before which lights are burning. On the Cross, the Saviour offered Himself for the whole world, so at the foot of the Cross we make ourselves one with Him and join our prayers with His. Crosses of prostration were common throughout the Celtic highlands and islands up to the last century, and the custom in the Eastern Church of expressing devotion to Christ without words, by touching the cross with the forehead, fits well with the Celtic emphasis on using all five senses in devotions. Meditative singing may precede the Prayer.

 A Prayer of Adoration

This or another prayer of adoration is used, with a sung response (R) after each sentence such as 'O Adoramus Te'.

Leader Lord Jesus Christ, High King of the Universe, you became as nothing to restore our lost innocence. *(R)*
You made your home on this earth, you overthrew the strongholds of Satan, and you freed those in dark prisons of sin. *(R)*
You are strong and gentle, and take the burdens of all who are broken or bruised. *(R)*
Suffering and victorious Champion of the poor, you open the gates of Heaven's Kingdom to all who call upon you. *(R)*

Words from the Bible

These sayings that Christ spoke from the Cross may be said, with a sung response (R) such as 'O Christe Domine Jesu' after each saying.

Leader Father forgive them; for they know not what they do. *(R)*
Truly I say to you today you will be with me in paradise. *(R)*
He is your son; she is your mother. *(R)*
My God, my God, why have you forsaken me?
I am thirsty. *(R)*
It is finished. *(R)*
Father, into your hands I commit my spirit. *(R)*

Or these Reproaches of Christ (adapted) with a sung response such as 'Mercy Lord, mercy Lord, have mercy Lord' after the words 'O my people' may be used.

Reader O my people, how have I offended you? Answer me.
I freed you from slavery;
Yet you handed me over to death and jeered at me.
O my people. *(R)*

I opened the sea before you;
You opened my side with a spear!
O my people. *(R)*

I moved before you in the pillar of cloud:
You led me to Pilate!
O my people. *(R)*

I watched over you in the desert and fed you with manna:
You struck me and scourged me!
O my people. *(R)*

I gave you from the rock living waters of salvation;
You gave me bitter drink, you quenched my thirst
with vinegar!
O my people. *(R)*

I struck down kings for you;
You struck me with a reed!
O my people. *(R)*

I put the sceptre into your hand and made you a
royal people;
You crowned me with the crown of thorns!
O my people. *(R)*

I made you great by my boundless power;
You hanged me on the gallows of the Cross!
O my people. *(R)*

All these things I have repeated in this your land;
Yet you have betrayed my sacrifice and spurned
my love!
O my people.

*Or there may be a Bible reading that records, presages
or reflects Christ's passion, followed by a sung
response.*

Silence

*At least ten minutes resting in Christ's presence
followed by meditative singing.*

Intercessions

*The leader should prepare intercessions on a theme
(including the Intercessions for Friday Evening
Worship) and each intercession should be followed by
a sung response. Other intercessions may then be
offered by anyone, with the same sung response, or an
Amen, after each.*

Devotion without words

The leader invites any who wish to kneel by the Cross and touch it with their foreheads or lips; this may be accompanied by quiet, meditative music, or singing in the Spirit, which may continue longer.

 ### Closing Prayers

One or more of these may be used here or after the silence.

Leader   On you was crucified the King of glory,
Sacrifice of Truth, Lamb without blemish,
His blood in streams downpouring;
On you was sacrificed the King of Kings,
His blood in streams downpouring.

May the Cross of Christ be over this face and this ear;
May the Cross of Christ be over this mouth and this throat;
May the Cross of Christ be over my arms,
From my shoulders to my hands.
May the Cross of Christ be with me, before me;
May the Cross of Christ be with me, behind me.
With the Cross of Christ may I meet every difficulty,
In the heights and in the depths.
From the top of my head to the tip of my toes,
I trust in the protection of your Cross, O Christ.

O Christ, you were put to death by cruel people who nailed you to a Cross; yet long before, you stretched out your arms in love to men, and women and children. May your way be our way, that we, too, may stretch out our arms in love to men, women and children.

O Christ of the tears, of the wounds, of the piercings,
May your Cross this night be shielding all.
Be your Cross between us and all enemies without;
Be your Cross between us and all enemies within;
Be your Cross our sure way from earth to heaven.

Saturday Evening Vigil of Fire

A fire was kept burning at all times in every church and monastery of Celtic Britain as a sign of God's presence; at the site of St Bridget's Convent in Kildare a fire was kept burning for a further thousand years. Today there is a longing for that fire of passionate Christian devotion to burst into flame again. The vigil is a way to kindle this.

People gather in a dark room around a living fire, or (in a church) an oil lamp or candle. As people gather there is either silence or singing of chants such as 'Kindle a flame'.

Leader　The Lord be with you.
　　All　And also with you.

Leader　Lord, sanctify this fire, and grant that this night we may burn with heavenly desires.

One or more of these or other sentences of Scripture is read.

Reader　One-third of the people shall be saved. This third I will bring into the fire; I will refine them like silver and test them like gold. They will call on my name and I will answer them; I will say 'They are my people', and they will say 'The Lord is our God'. (*Zechariah 13:8, 9*)

The messenger you desire will come . . . he will be like a refining fire. (*Malachi 3:1, 2*)

(John the Baptist said) One greater than I will come who will baptise you with the Holy Spirit and with fire. (*Luke 33:16*)

(Jesus said) I have come to bring fire on the earth. (*Luke 12:49*)

When the day of Pentecost came, all the believers were gathered together in one place. . . . Then they saw what looked like tongues of fire which spread out and touched each person there. They were all filled with the Holy Spirit. (*Acts 2:1, 3*)

 Prayer

Leader   Eternal Creator of day and night, as darkness deepens, and we look for your coming, cleanse us by your refining fire; dispel the darkness of our hearts, and kindle in us the pentecostal flame.

 Psalm 97

All   A fire prepares God's path.

Leader   The Lord is King, let earth rejoice, let all the coastlands be glad.
Cloud and darkness are God's raiment; God's throne is justice and right.

All   A fire prepares God's path.

Leader   A fire prepares God's path, it burns all that opposes God on every side.
God's lightning lights up the world, the earth trembles at the sight.

All   A fire prepares God's path.

Leader	The mountains melt like wax before the Lord of all the earth. The skies proclaim his justice; all peoples see his glory.
All	A fire prepares God's path.
Leader	Let those who serve idols be ashamed, those who boast of their worthless gods. All you spirits worship the Lord.
All	A fire prepares God's path.
Leader	For you indeed are the Lord, most high above all the earth, exalted far above all spirits.
All	A fire prepares God's path.
Leader	The Lord loves those who hate evil; the Lord guards the souls of his saints; he sets them free from the wicked.
All	A fire prepares God's path.
Leader	Light shines forth for the just, and joy for the upright of heart. Rejoice, you just, in the Lord; give glory to God's holy name.
All	A fire prepares God's path.

There may be singing of songs or chants on the theme of the glory of God.

One of these or other passages from Scripture or Celtic writings may be read:

Reader	*Luke 24:13–32.*

From the Confession of St Patrick:

Reader	The love and fear of God increased more and more in me and my faith began to grow, and my spirit to be stirred up, so that in one day I would say as many as a hundred prayers and nearly as many

at night, even when I was staying out in the woods or on the mountain. And I used to rise before dawn for prayer, in snow and frost and rain, and I used to feel no ill effect and there was no slackness in me. I now realise it was because the Spirit was glowing in me.

The main part of the vigil, which follows, usually takes the form of silent prayer. The silence may be followed by a litany, prepared intercessions or the repetition of the Jesus Prayer ('Lord Jesus Christ, have mercy on me, a sinner'). The Gospel reading for the Sunday service may be read and reflected upon.

The following or another hymn is sung:

All   O thou who camest from above,
The pure celestial fire to impart,
Kindle a flame of sacred love,
On the mean altar of my heart.

There let it for thy glory burn,
In inextinguishable blaze;
And trembling to its source return,
In humble prayer and fervent praise.

Jesus, confirm my heart's desire,
To work and speak and think for thee;
Still let me guard the holy fire,
And still stir up thy gift in me.

Ready for all thy perfect will,
My acts of faith and love repeat,
Till death thy endless mercies seal,
And make the sacrifice complete.

One or both of these prayers may be said:

Leader   King of the sun, without beginning, without time,
O Son of the loveliest Mary, from the lowest of all
to the Name that is highest of all,
Kindle in my heart a flame of love to my
neighbour, and to my foe, a flame of love to the
brave, to the knave, to all; O Son of the loveliest
Mary.

Kindle in our hearts, O God, the flame of that love
which never ceases, that it may burn in us, giving
light to others.
May we shine for ever in your temple,
Set on fire with your eternal light,
Even your Son Jesus Christ,
Our Saviour and our Redeemer.

Let us go in the undying fire of his love.
All   Thanks be to God.

Silence is kept until morning.

Five Night Prayers, or Night Caps

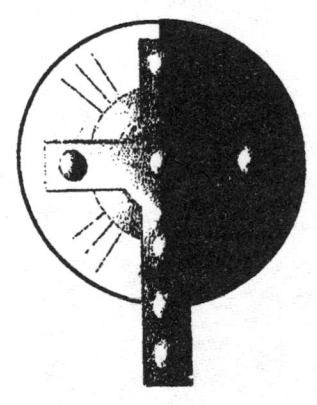

The old word for the prayers that were said together last thing at night was 'Compline', meaning 'that which completes the day'. More recently that has been replaced by the term 'Night Prayer'. I think 'Night Cap' better carries the original meaning.

In formal Christian communities, silence is often kept after this service until breakfast. Those who live alone or in a household with other like-minded people, or those who make a retreat together, might also find this a helpful practice at times.

General Theme

Leader   ✝ In the name of the restful Father,
In the name of the calming Son,
In the name of the peaceful Spirit,
May we and God be one.

Leader   I place my soul and body
Under your guarding this night, O God,
O Father of help to frail pilgrims,
Protector of heaven and earth.

All   I place my soul and body
Under your guiding this night, O Christ,
O Son of the tears and the piercings,
May your Cross this night be my shield.

Leader   I place my soul and body
Under your glowing this night, O Spirit,
O gentle Companion, and soul Guardian,
My heart's eternal Warmth.

Psalm 134 or another Psalm may be sung or said. It may be sung once, hummed once, and sung again:

All   Come bless the Lord, all you servants of the Lord,
Who stand by night in the house of the Lord;
Lift up your hands in the holy place,
Come bless the Lord, come bless the Lord.

Leader   May that part of me that did not grow at morning,
Grow at nightfall . . .

Short pause. On appropriate occasions withdrawals or compromises of the day may be named silently or aloud and placed at Christ's feet – the place of at-one-ment.

Leader   You are our Saviour and Lord;
All   In our stumbling be our Shield.

Leader   In our tiredness be our Rest;
All   In our darkness be our Light.

Reader   O Christ, Son of the living God,
May your holy angels guard our sleep.
May they watch over us as we rest
And hover around our beds.

Reader   Let them reveal to us in our dreams
Visions of your glorious truth,
O High Prince of the universe,
O High Priest of the mysteries.

Reader   May no dreams disturb our rest
And no nightmares darken our dreams.
May no fears or worries delay
Our willing, prompt repose.

These or other words of Christ may be read:

Reader   Come to me, all you who are weary and burdened, and I will give you rest. Take my yoke upon you and learn from me, for I am gentle and humble of heart, and you will find rest for your souls.
(Matthew 11:28, 29)

This may be followed by silence during which other words from God may be spoken spontaneously . . .

Leader   My dear ones bless, O God, and keep in every
          place where they are, especially. . . .

          Anyone may repeat this: Gerry + Monica.

    Any   . . .

    All   May the great and strong heavenly army encircle
            them all with their outstretched arms;
            To protect them from the hostile powers;
            To put balm into their dreams;
            To give them contented, sweet repose.

Leader   I lie down this night with God,
    All   And God will lie down with me;

Leader   I lie down this night with Christ,
    All   And Christ will lie down with me;

Leader   I lie down this night with the Spirit,
    All   And the Spirit will lie down with me;

Leader   God and Christ and the Spirit,
    All   Lying down with me.

          All say together (or each may say in turn):

    All   I make the sign of the Cross of Christ, ✠
            My Christ, my Shield, my Encircler;
            Each day, each night, in light, in dark,
            My Treasure, my dear One.

            The almighty and merciful Three encircle us, that
            awake we may watch with Christ, and asleep we
            may rest in peace.

Brigid Theme

Leader   I am under the keeping
Of the Friend of Brigid:
Early and late,
Each dark, each light.

I make Christ's Cross over my eyes ☩

All   I make Christ's Cross over my eyes ☩

Leader   Each day and each night
That I place myself under Christ's keeping:

All   I shall not be forgotten;
I shall not be destroyed;
I shall not be imprisoned;
I shall not be harassed by evil powers.

Leader   Nightmares shall not lie on me.
All   Black thoughts shall not lie on me.
Leader   No ill-will shall lie on me.

Reader   *Psalm 16:1–3, 7–11 or verses from another Psalm.*

Leader   Keep me as the apple of your eye.
All   Hide me under the shadow of your wings.

Silence.

Reader   *John 15:1–5a.*

Each of these petitions may be followed by a pause:

Leader   May I abide in Christ.
Reader   May the fruits God gave Brigid lie on me . . .
Reader   May the delights God gave Brigid lie on me . . .

Reader   May the healings God gave Brigid lie on me . . .
Reader   May the virtues God gave Brigid lie on me . . .
Reader   May the peace God gave Brigid lie on me . . .

Leader   May these blessings lie also on our loved ones.
          We remember especially . . .

          Loved ones may be silently recalled or named aloud.

Any   . . .

There may be singing.

Leader   Ever shielding Father,
          Ever loving Son,
          Life-giving Holy Spirit,
          Ever Three in One:
          Rain grace on us and heal us
          And we shall lie down in peace.
All   Rain grace on us and heal us
          And we shall lie down in peace

RESURRECTION Theme

Leader   ✠ In the name of the joyful Father,
In the name of the rising Sun,
In the name of the life-giving Spirit,
In the name of the Three-in-One.

We rejoice in the rising of Christ from death:

All   This night we will lie down in his joy and peace!

Reader   *Read Psalm 118:15–24, or Psalm 126, or from the Psalm for the day.*

Leader   (*or males*) This night, O Victor over death:
Raise me from the death of denial;
Raise me from the death of fear;
Raise me from the death of despair.

Reader   (*or females*) This night, O Victor over death:
Wake me to the eternal 'Yes';
Wake me to the rays of Hope;
Wake me to the light of Dawn.

𝄞   *There may be singing.*

Reader   *This reading from John 20:19–20 or 1 Peter 3:18, 22; 2 Corinthians 4:11–16 or another reading from the New Testament may be read.*

On the evening of the first day of the week, when the disciples were together, with the doors locked for fear of the Jews, Jesus came and stood among them and said 'Peace be with you!' After he said this he showed them his hands and his side. The disciples were overjoyed when they saw the Lord.

Leader We lie down in peace knowing our sins are forgiven;
All   We lie down in peace knowing death has no fear.

Leader We lie down in peace knowing no powers can harm us;
All   We lie down in peace knowing angels are near.

Leader Risen Christ of the scars, who spoke peace to your desolate disciples,
        Speak peace this night to us and to desolate ones we love.

Reader Risen Christ of the lakeside, who nourished and inspired your disciples,
        Inspire us and our loved ones to rest this night in your arms.
        We especially remember:
Any   (mention names) . . .

There may be singing, music, silence or free prayer.

Leader Risen Christ, watch over us this night
        And keep us in the light of your presence.
        May our praise continually blend
        With the song of all creation.

All   Deep peace of the setting sun;
        Deep peace of the forgiving heart;
        Deep peace of the lakeside Christ
        Be ours, tonight, for ever.

Leader The eye of the Risen Christ be upon us as we sleep;
        The eye of affection and mercy;
        The eye of joy and gladness;
        Bringing to dawn our wholeness.

Pentecost Theme

Leader   ✛ In the name of the Father of poor folk;
          In the name of the King of the gifts;
          In the name of the flaming Spirit.

          Holy Spirit, Power of powers, come to us this night;
          Holy Spirit, Joy of joys, sing praise with us this
          night;
          Holy Spirit, Strengthener, grow strong in us this
          night.

Reader   *Psalm 139:1–12 or verses from another Psalm.*

          Flame of love
All   Light us up.
Reader   Flame of beauty
All   Light us up.
Reader   Flame of wisdom
All   Light us up.
Reader   Flame of peace,
All   Light us up.

Leader   May the colours of this day fill up our night,
          and the rays of God's Son bring peace to our dawn.

          May the virtue of our daily work
          Hallow our nightly prayers.
          May our sleep be deep and soft,
          So our work be fresh and hard.

There may be singing.

Reader   *Ephesians 4:2–4 or other verses from the New Testament.*

Leader   Rest like dew on the peoples of the world,
And on all whom we have met this day.
Rest like dew on my tired soul,
And on all the loved ones we name.

Any   *Loved ones may be named . . .*

Leader   Where day is breaking,
Where dark is overshadowing,
Where souls are wounded,

All   Come with your balm,
Restore with your Spirit,
Baptise with your love.

Leader   Holy Three our dwelling be,
Creator, Saviour, Spirit dear.

*An angel figure from
the Book of Kells*

Michaelmas Theme

Leader   Let us lay aside the cares of the day, that we,
like the angels, who neither fret nor fear,
may offer worship, and rest in the joy of the Lord.

A silence follows for reflection on the past day.

Leader   Thrice holy is the Three of limitless love.
All   Holy God,
Holy and strong,
Holy and immortal,
Have mercy on us.

Leader   Have mercy on us, O God, for our sins; may these
and the things of this day which have clogged our
lives now fall away from us.
The light of the angels be ours;
The joy of the angels be ours;
The peace of the angels be ours.

 Singing

Reader   *Psalm 91:1–12. Response after every two verses:*

All   God's angels guard you in all your ways.

Reader   *Revelation 21:9–12.*

Reader   O angel guardian of my right hand,
Attend to me this night;
Rescue me from battling floods;
Array me in your clothes, for I am naked,
Succour me, for I am feeble and forlorn.

Reader   Guard me in the treacherous turnings
And save me from harm this night.
Drive from me the taint of pollution;
Encompass me till death, from evil.
O kindly angel of my right hand
Deliver me this night!

Reader   O Michael militant, king of the angels,
Shield your people with the power of your sword.
Spread your wing over sea and land
And shield us from the foe.
O Michael of militance, Michael of wounding,
Shield me from the grudge
Of ill-wishers this night.

*There may be singing or spontaneous words of
scripture.*

Leader   Lord, may your protecting peace be upon those we
love.
Your protecting peace be upon *N——.*

Anyone may repeat this prayer for a named person.

Any   Your protecting peace be upon. . . .

Leader   May angels watch over our dreams.

Leader   Now we will lie down in peace.
Now we will sleep in God.
All   Now we will sleep in God.

May the seven angels of the Holy Spirit
And the two guardian angels
Shield us this and every night,
Till light and dawn shall come.

A Celtic
Holy Communion

A Celtic
holy Communion

 There may be singing.

Leader Let this wondrous creation, plundered by alien forces, open wide its arms to its returning Saviour. Let all the people, marked with the Creator's dignity, welcome him who comes to restore our lost innocence.

Reader As the birds brought food to your people in the parched deserts, so now you bring food to our parched and hungry souls.

There may be singing. Anyone or designated persons may speak out good things about God or God's creation. At longer gatherings there may be dancing, creative arts, eating or sharing of news.

Lamentation

Reader As we draw near to the place of at-one-ment:
Give us tears to see the wonder of your presence;
Give us tears to see the wasting of your people;
Give us tears to see the wounding of your Son.

All We are the race that helped make the wood on which you were crucified, and still we misuse your creation;
We are the race that helped make the nails that pierced your body, yet still we use work for gain at others' expense;

We are the race that did nothing to stop your
betrayers, yet still we are ruled by comfort or
cowardice.

Reader   Mercy Lord, mercy Lord, have mercy Lord.
All   Mercy Lord, mercy Lord, have mercy Lord.

(or sing 'Kyrie, Kyrie, eleison' three times)

*Silence. During this, anyone, or designated persons,
may speak out hurts, pains, or sorrows with which they
or the world around is oppressed. This concludes with
'Mercy Lord', or 'Kyrie', being repeated. A priest may
pronounce absolution or the following words may be
said:*

Leader   O soul be joyful;
The saving God stretches out His hand to you
To announce a loving reconciliation.
Washed and made whole, let us open our hearts to
God in prayer.

The Word of God

*The prayer and readings for the day, or any of the
following, may be used.*

Leader   Grant, O Lord, that your church in this land may
be true to its birthright. Kindle in us the adventure
of obedience, the single eye, the humble ways, the
generous spirit which marked Aidan and your
Celtic saints.

Reader   *Isaiah 6:1–8 or the Old Testament reading for the day.*

Singing

Reader   *Colossians 3:8–17 or the New Testament reading for
the day.*

If there is also to be a reading from a Gospel, silence should precede it.

Reader *Matthew 11:25–30 or the Gospel reading for the day.*

Singing, silence, teaching, creative activities, prayer or sharing of words from God.

 Creative Activity

Prepare prayers, pictures, incense, candles or other signs of devotion to be brought up with the bread, wine and gifts of money.

The Peace

Leader Peace in your thinking. Peace in your hearts.
Peace with creation. Peace with one another.
The peace of Christ be with you.

All The peace of Christ be with you.

Leader Let us greet one another with these words of peace.

The Offering

During a song, offerings may be collected: bread, wine, money, and any items prepared during the Creative Activity.

Leader Now let us lay aside all cares of this life, that we, like the angels, may offer our worship, joining with them in singing to the thrice-holy and life-giving Trinity:

All sing or say:

All Holy, holy, holy is the Lord, holy is the Lord God Almighty! *(twice)*
Who was, and is, and is to come!
Holy, holy, holy is the Lord!

Glory to . . .

The following may be omitted if the prayers were said earlier. It should be said by a female if the leader is male, or vice versa:

Reader   We bless you, High King of all creation. Through your goodness we have this bread and wine to offer, which earth has given and human hands have made; they will become our spiritual food and drink.

All   Blessed be God for ever.

Reader   As we bring this bread to you *(lift up the bread)* we offer you the sap of life rising; our energies and all that we create; the fun, the relationships, and the communications of life.

We pour out this wine *(pour out the wine)* and offer to you the woes of life outpouring; the waning powers, disease and disappointments; hurts and handicaps. As grapes are crushed to make the wine, so we offer to you all who are crushed by hunger or homelessness, violence or abuse. You who put beam in sun and moon, take all this, and transform it into the deep, rich wine of everlasting life.

The Thanksgiving

Leader   Lift up your hearts.
All   We lift them to the Lord.

Leader   Let us thank the Lord for all He has done.
All   God leads His people through the years.

Leader   High King of the universe, you brought forth the earth; you breathe wisdom into all your creatures, till we reflect your Three-fold friendship. In our pain and sorrow we cry out to you, tender Lamb, slain before the world began, perfect sacrifice for our sins.

By the power of your Holy Spirit may these gifts of bread and wine be for us Christ's body and blood

who, on the night He was betrayed, took bread,
gave you thanks, broke it and gave it to His
disciples saying: Take, eat, this is my body which is
given for you. After supper He took the cup, gave
you thanks, and said to them: Drink, all of you;
this is my blood of the new covenant which is shed
for you and for many for the forgiveness of sins.
Do this in remembrance of me.

Reader   Alas, we have seen the Son of the living God
stretched out on a Cross;
Alas, the body that possesses wisest dignity has
been plunged into blood; a crown of thorns placed
about His beauteous head.
The blood of Christ is flowing through His
gleaming sides.
This Cross is like the parting of the day from night.
Yet through it, all may now proclaim:

All   Christ has died!
Christ is risen!
Christ will come again!

Leader   Risen Christ we welcome you. You are the
flowering bough of creation; from you cascades
music like a million stars, truth to cleanse a
myriad souls. From you flee demons, omens and
all ill-will; around you rejoice the angels of light.
Father, send us the tender Spirit of the Lamb;
Feed us with the Bread of Heaven;
May we become drunk with your holiness.

Communion

followed by singing.

Leader   Heaven is intertwined with earth. Alleluia!
We have taken the divine life into ourselves.
Alleluia!
And so now each may say:

All	I rise up clothed in the strength of Christ.
	I shall not be imprisoned, I shall not be harmed;
	I shall not be down-trodden, I shall not be left alone;
	I shall not be tainted, I shall not be overwhelmed.
	I go clothed in Christ's white garments;
	I go freed to weave Christ's patterns;
	I go loved to serve Christ's weak ones;
	I go armed to rout out Christ's foes.
Leader	The saving streams from the pierced heart of Christ save you.
	The Sacred Three shield you from all ill-will; protect you from all that destroys; and lead you always along Christ's paths.
	Go in peace to love and serve the Lord.
All	In the name of Christ. Amen.

Note for Church of England clergy

Here is an example of how the Celtic Holy Communion may be integrated with the Order for Holy Communion Rite A in the *Alternative Service Book 1980* of the Church of England.

Before the ministers arrive

The ASB only provides for worship after the ministers arrive. In the ancient catholic and apostolic church the people gathered for informal fellowship and worship before this.[7] Free use of fresh material may be welcomed before the formal arrival of ministers.

The Preparation

ASB 1–3: 'The president welcomes the people using these or other appropriate words'. The opening section of the Celtic Holy Communion may be used.

Prayers of Penitence

ASB 4–11: 'Alternative confessions may be used'. The second section of the Celtic Holy Communion, Lamentation, may be used.

The Ministry of the Word

ASB 12–19: The third section in the Celtic Holy Communion, The Word of God, meets all requirements. Note that bishops now encourage a variety of 'Affirmations of Faith' such as are provided in the *ASB* baptism service and in *Patterns of Worship*. The Nicene Creed or the Creed before the New Testament reading for Morning Worship for Saturdays may be used.

The Intercession, the Peace, the Preparation of Gifts

ASB 20–35: The fourth section in the Celtic Holy Communion, The Offering, and The Peace which precedes this, meet all requirements.

The Eucharistic Prayer

ASB 36–49: Words from section five of The Celtic Holy Communion, The Thanksgiving, may be inserted before the prescribed Eucharistic Prayers, at the Proper Preface, or after it. When using the Celtic Holy Communion, Church of England clergy should bear in mind that sections 42, 43 and 45 of the *ASB* should be said, with the proviso that 'the minister may use variations which are not of substantial importance in any form of service. . . .'

After Communion

ASB 50–56: 'An appropriate sentence . . . or other suitable prayers may be said.' The final section of the Celtic Eucharist, Blessings, may be used.

Some Special
Celebrations

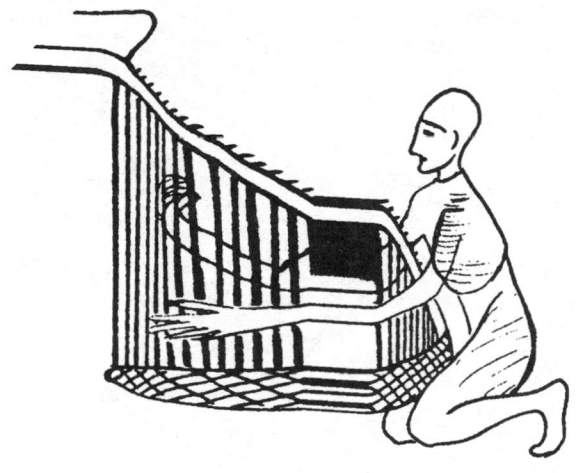

Evening Worship
for the Winter Solstice
21st December

 In darkest day we look to the Lord of dark and light

People gather in an open place after dark around a fire. If possible hot food, drink and music should be provided at a nearby building which may be decorated with holly and ivy. Those who have no heavy duty the next day may stay up until the early hours, enjoying the sights and sounds of the night. This liturgy may begin the celebration or be used at any appropriate time. The opening voices of leader and reader should be male and female.

Leader   ✠ In the name of the Lord of the solstice.
In the name of the Lord of the dark.
In the name of the Spirit of the mysteries.

Reader   Christ at every beginning.
Christ at every end.
Christ at the yearly turning.
Christ at every bend.

Leader   Christ in dark's deep shadows.
Christ in shades of death.
Christ in primeval history.
Christ in wintry earth.

The Word of God

Reader   *Psalm 139:1–16 or Psalm 18.*

         There may be singing that reflects the mystery of God and of the creation.

Leader   Creator of the universe, infinite and glorious;
         You give us laws to save us from our folly.
         Give us eyes to see your plan unfolding,
         Your purpose emerging as the world is made.

Reader   Let us attend, the Word of God comes to us.
All   Thanks be to God.

Reader   Illumine our hearts, O Lord, implant in us a desire for your truth; may all that is false within us flee. Hear the Word of God from the Old Testament in Isaiah 45:1–8.

         The reading.

Reader   This is the Word of the Lord.
All   Thanks be to God.

The world is not dead

Leader   The world is not dead:
All   It is sleeping.

Leader   Its life draws in:
All   It is keeping.

Leader   The earth is gathering energy:
All   For a new burst of life.

Leader   We breathe in the mystic air:
All   That we may breathe out care.

Leader   Your presence supports us through the night:
All   So we can hail the coming source of Light.

Leader   Shine through the mists, the deadening heavy clod:
All   Hail gladdening Light of God's pure glory poured.

Reader	Let us attend. Christ the living Word comes to us. Hear the Word of Christ from the New Testament in John 1:1–14.
All	Praise to Christ our Lord.

Prayers

Reader	Lord, this night is a sacrament. In the darkness we do not depend upon our own powers to control our destiny; we become aware that we depend upon what is given by you. We become aware that we are frail, that we need to become wise, and respectful of hidden dangers. Tonight we cannot be over-familiar with our Creator; tonight we need your Presence to conquer fear. Tonight respect and awe are restored to their rightful place.
Leader	Lord of the seasons, on this day of briefest light, help us to be at home with the treasures of the dark. . . .

Pause during which anyone may mention examples.

As the days have drawn in, help us to flow with the ebb tides of life.

Pause during which anyone may mention examples.

As shadows lengthen, help us to embrace the shadow side of life.

Pause during which anyone may mention examples.

At the turning of the year, help us to welcome the Dawn from on high.

Reader	Now begins the twelve long nights of yule. One night soon will be born Jesus, Son of the King of Glory, creation's Joy. You will gleam to Him moon and furthest stars. You will gleam to Him hills and housetops afar.

All   Glow to Him wood and tree,
Glow to Him moon and sun,
Glow to Him earth and air,
Glow to Him water and fire,
Glow to Him people at night,
When earth's Glory comes to reign.

Sensing the Elements

Each person may go to a space in the open where they try to sense the mystery of the dark, the rhythm of the seasons, the energy of the earth, the glory of the elements. It may be possible to touch a tree and feel its breathing; to feel the flow of life beginning to move in the earth. Listen to what is there. Reach out to welcome all that it is to bring forth. Meditate upon, offer to God, and bless the four elements in turn: the earth, the air, the fire, the water. When you are ready, return to the fire and the food. There may be dancing in a circle to mirror the circle of the coming sun. Before people begin to go home, everyone holds hands in a circle, walks in the direction of the sun (east to west) and prays this prayer.

The Circle

All   Circle me Lord,
Keep light and love within,
Keep dark powers and demons without.

Circle me Lord,
Keep health and hope within,
Keep depression and denial without.

Circle me Lord,
Keep childlike trust within,
Keep fear of death's powers without.

Leader   The Holy Three encircling be,
Nurturing in eternity.

All   Giving more than we can ask,
Scattering darkness from our path.

An Alternative Christmas

 In our western society the 'Christmas spirit' has become diseased, and whole neighbourhoods can be taken over by a godless mentality, which infects churches, too. Increasing numbers of people are so marginalised at Christmas that they boycott it altogether, or turn to drink, violence or suicide.

We may be sure the Celtic church celebrated the Nativity of God's Son with wonder, simplicity, and with a flare for making Bethlehem 'present' in each locality. The following is a way of celebrating the Nativity which may be adopted both by those who boycott the conventional Christmas and by those who simply want to deepen their experience of Christmas.

On Christmas Eve or earlier a crib is placed in a communal meeting place or church, and a candle is lit in front of the infant Christ. A silent vigil for prayer is arranged all day until midnight. In front of the crib is a place where people can place and light a candle, and a basket where they can place a prayer to Jesus.

Either then, or preferably on the 'Day of Joy' itself, each person brings a gift to Jesus and leaves it in front of the crib. Gifts may include: a tin of money collected for a needy cause; a flower, prayer, card, or written promise; a song, poem, dance, painting, photograph or crafted object; or something beautiful from God's creation. When numbers present are sufficient, intersperse the offering of gifts with Bible readings, singing, music, or poetry.

Vigil Prayers at the Crib

*Each line of each prayer may be used for several
minutes' meditation.*

Jesus, we kneel before you in silent amazement.
Thank you that, because of your birth, we know
that our Father is with us.
May we welcome you, not in a cold manger of a
heart,
But in a heart so pure, a heart warm with love for
one another.

Jesus you are –
The tender holy Babe;
The Shepherd of your flock;
The Healing Person;
The Christ of the people;
The world-pervading God;
Emmanuel, God-with-us.

We'll kiss your hands,
We'll dry your feet with our hair.
And Jesus, never forsake us.

Jesus, you are –
The Glory of eternity who now shines among us;
Son of the High King of the universe;
Splendour of the Father;
Source of life;
Prince of Peace;
Wonderful Counsellor;
Son of Mary;
Pattern of goodness;
Friend of all;
Brother of the poor;
Champion of justice;
Joy of angels.

Jesus, in you we see God's face –
Gentle;
Smiling;
Strong;
Loving;
Obedient.

Jesus, you radiate what the world so needs today –
Gentleness, tenderness, light and hope.

In you, may we find –
Gentleness as the answer to violence;
Tenderness as the answer to ill-will;
Light as the answer to lies;
Hope as the answer to despair.

Infant Jesus —
Truly God, truly human,
Truly infinite, truly frail.
Your greatness holds the universe;
Your lovely countenance attracts our hearts;
Your goodness beckons all that is good in us;
Your wisdom searches us;
Your truth sheds light on our darkness;
Your generosity enriches our poverty;
Your friendship consoles the unwanted;
Your strength turns away all evils;
Your justice deters wrong-doing;
Your power conquers hell;
Your love-enflamed heart kindles our cold hearts;
Your miraculous hand fills us with all blessings;
Your sweet and holy name rejoices all who love you;
Your mercy brings forgiveness.
Have mercy on us, bring us to true sorrow for our
sins,
Give us eternal life.
For your glory fills eternity;
your glory fills the universe.

Christmas Eve Prayer Walk

For a household (the household can be extended to include relatives, friends, neighbours).

Go for a walk in the streets around your neighbourhood, imagining you are Mary and Joseph looking for a warm place to stay until their baby is born. Pray that the people in each house you pass will open the doors of their hearts to Jesus and His family this Christmas.

On your return home, place a crib in a shed, garage or foyer. Light a candle, and say this prayer:

Homemaker God,
Come this night to all who are sleeping rough;
Come to the cardboard huts and the dampened squats;
Come to the young who have lost their way;
Come to the old who have been forgotten.
May the light of the Bethlehem stable be a light to the homeless tonight. Amen.

Now go inside into the warmth of your main living room. Take the crib (or have a second crib) in this room. Read the story of the birth of Jesus from Luke 2:4–20. Then each person may pick up one of the crib figures and tell what that person means to them. At the end of this, write some prayers and place these, or other items of affection, in the crib.

Go to the window. While one person holds a candle, another reads John 1:1–14.

Say together:

Now is born Christ the King of greatness:
Now is the time of the great Nativity.
Glow to Him wood and tree;
Glow to Him mount and sea;
Glow to Him land and plain;
Come to Him, people, and let Him reign.

*Now proclaim the light of Christ to the world, facing
the window, and holding the candle high, one person
leading, the others responding:*

Leader   God is light:
All   In whom is no darkness at all.

Leader   Christ is the light of the world:
All   A light no darkness can quench.

*The head of the family concludes by introducing a
sharing of the Christmas peace:*

The Son of Mary is the Prince of peace. May the
peace of our Saviour Jesus be with each of us this
Christmas season.

*Share Christmas greetings with hugs, kisses, mince
pies, drinks, presents etc!*

New Year

For use at home or in church at any time between New Year's Eve and Epiphany (6th January).

A crib is placed in the front. Three people each bring up a figure of a king as indicated. These actions and prayers may be interwoven with teaching and singing.

Leader I said to the man who stood at the gate of the year: 'Give me a light that I may tread safely into the unknown'. And he replied: 'Go out into the darkness and put your hand into the hand of God. That shall be to you better than light and safer than a known way.'

As tides recede we plant fresh footprints on the sand;
As white flakes fall we print fresh marks on untrod snow;
As a new year dawns we walk afresh on virgin ground.
Let us learn from the wise kings of the long journey about how our journey should be.

The figure of the first king bearing gold is placed in the crib (everyone may follow and kneel by the crib each time this is done).

Leader We offer our gold, our prosperity, our possessions; all that we have. We offer our power, our roles to you. We let go of the things we cling to. We bring our emptiness, our hopes . . .

Silence or free prayer; recorded verses of the hymn 'Rock of Ages' may be listened to.

A volunteer places the figure of the incense-bearing king in the crib.

Leader   We offer our mind-sets to Christ; our past, our conditioning, the stereotypes that we inherit or acquire; our churchmanship, our hobby-horses . . . And we place them at His disposal.

Incense may be lit.

Leader   Lord, forgive us for trying to control you and the way things work in your world. We open ourselves to you, ready to be filled with your Presence as incense fills a holy place.

Silence or music. A volunteer brings the figure of the myrrh-bearing king and places it in the crib.

Leader   We offer the shadows of our lives, the sadness, the things that are crushed; we offer you our little deaths and our final death. These are like the straw in the stable; may something beautiful for you be born in all of this straw.

The leader goes to the front or altar, lights and holds a candle, and prays this Journey Prayer:

Leader   Be a smooth way before me,
Be a guiding star above me,
Be a keen eye behind me,
This day, this year, for ever.

The leader walks with the candle to the doorway and gives this Blessing:

Leader   God be with you at every leap;
         Christ be with you on every steep;
         Spirit be with you in every deep;
         Each step of the journey you go.

Easter Eve Vigil

 This should begin after dark. A prayer vigil may precede or follow it. In some places people bring sleeping bags and carry on a vigil throughout the night. A fire is lit outside (or if this is difficult a Calor Gas fire inside). People gather inside within sight of the fire. Various traditions provide an Easter garden, an empty cross, or even a draped coffin as the indoor focus of the gathering. A supply of pencils and paper, of small individual candles, and an unlit Easter candle will be required.

Introduction

Leader   Sisters and Brothers in Christ, on this night in which our Lord Jesus Christ passed over from death to life, we gather in prayer with God's waiting people throughout the world beside a flame which will be for us a Fire of Memorial, a Fire of Purifying and the Fire of the Risen Christ.

The resurrection of Christ is the promise of our own resurrection, which already begins invisibly here on earth. We celebrate this with our Service of Light, which is a sign of our identity as children of the Light. We shall declare the victory of Christ over the powers of darkness which still pervade our neighbourhood and nation.

A Fire of Memorial

Leader   May this fire of memorial rekindle in us the memory and the mourning of his death.

Leader	We recall the grieving women of Galilee who brought spices to adorn Christ's body in the tomb. May we, too, express our devotion: by offering a token of our love.
	Anyone may place a flower, perfume or keepsake by the tomb (if there is an Easter Garden) or by a Cross,
Leader (contd)	Or by our silent presence here, and by saying together:
All	O King of the Friday, Whose limbs were stretched on the Cross, O Lord who did suffer The bruises, the wounds, the loss. We stretch ourselves beneath the shield of your might; Some fruit from the tree of your passion Fall on us this night! *(Irish)*
Leader	Now let us hear words spoken about the One we mourn by His friends or admirers, as recorded in the Bible:

Readers:

A   No one ever loved as he loved.

B   Someone might lay down their life for a person who did them good: but He laid down His life for those who did only bad to Him.

C   We were amazed: never did anyone speak as He spoke. He spoke with authority.

D   He knew everything about me.

E   We observed Him, we were with Him, He was full of grace and truth.

F   We were drawn to Him alone, because He alone had the words of eternal life.

G   He was the voice of the poor, of the dispossessed, who cried: 'Come to me, all you who are loaded with heavy burdens.'

H He cried over our city 'How often I would have gathered you to me as a hen gathers her chicks, but you would not heed me. Now it is too late.'

Leader We mourn a life of such goodness, cut down in its flower.
We mourn for a people who forfeited the flowering of their destiny.
We mourn for a city which turned away from its Saviour.
We mourn for a planet which rejected its Maker.
We mourn for ourselves, who languish, alone and lost.

All Lord, we offer you –
Our tears,
The spices of our faith,
The ointment of our tenderness,
The flowers of our personality,
The memories of your life.

 Singing

A song about Christ dying on the Cross. Paper and pencils are distributed during or after the singing.

 Reading

Reader *Exodus 14:19–31.*

A Fire of Purification

Leader Before the celebration of the Passover can begin in a Jewish household every corner has to be spotlessly cleaned. We bring before the Lord, the unclean things that drive His world, and this neighbourhood, far from Him. We ask that the fire of His holiness may purge us of all these things, and that the purging may sweep through this land.

Lord, for –

All Arrogance that pretends we are self-sufficient;
Prejudice and contempt towards others;
Our abuse and mistreatment of your creation;
The mindless use of products that pollute;
Grudges, resentment, and our failure to forgive;
Peddling of gossip, taking sides and building up
walls of resentment;
Cynicism and devaluing that which is good;
Selfish ambition and misuse of others for profit;
Imposing unnecessary restless activity upon your
day of rest;
Worship of money and created things rather than
you, Creator;
Abuse and exploitation of your sexual gifts;
Failure to protect the lives of the unwanted and
the unborn.
Forgive us, O Lord, and burn out these things from
our lives, our locality, and our land, we pray.

 Creative activity

*There may be a period of silence in which to confess
personal sins. Write down anything on pieces of paper.
When the leader indicates, take these to the fire. After
a short silence, place the papers on the fire:*

Leader Through Christ's victorious death your sins are
forgiven and you are cleansed. Through Christ's
descent into the world of the dead even
imprisoned spirits were set free. Let us raise high
the Cross and proclaim this victory of Christ:

All The victory of the Cross over the evils of the past
and the evil powers of the present.
The victory of the Cross over the strongholds of
death, fear and disease.

The victory of the Cross over poverty and apathy, hatred and division.
The victory of the Cross in heaven, on earth, and here in this place.

Return inside.

Hymn

'Christ harrows hell' by Brother Ramon SSF.
Tune: Gonfalon Royal.

Now while the body, quiet and still
Lies wrapped in bands of linen fair
The glow of life and warmth and power
Flickers in hell's cold darkling air.

And while the myrrh and aloes' balm
Perfume his feet and hands and head
Christ's spreading light pierces the gloom
And lights the kingdom of the dead.

The doors of bronze burst at his cry
And all the sons of Adam wake;
He harrows hell and breaks death's bonds
And all the powers of darkness shake.

Adam and Eve, that primal pair
Are led on high to liberty;
While patriarch and prophet stand
And sing the song of jubilee.

The dying thief beholds his Lord
Fulfilled the promise of the King;
While saints of that first covenant
Join with angelic choirs and sing.

The breaking of the Easter dawn
Reveals the body of the Lord
Endued with life and love and power
Incarnate is the eternal Word.

All glory, Christ, our risen King
Who with the Father reigns above
Within the Holy Spirit's bond
Eternal Life and Light and Love.

Leader This is the night when you saved our forebears in the faith:
You freed the people of Israel from their slavery and led them dry-shod through the sea. This is the night when the pillar of fire destroyed the darkness of sin.

This is the night when Christ, the true Lamb, is slain, whose blood consecrates the homes of all believers. This is the night when Jesus Christ broke the chains of sin and death and rose triumphant from the grave. What good would life have been to us if Christ had not come as our Redeemer?

This is the night when Christians everywhere, washed clean of sin and freed from all that degrades them, are restored to grace and grow together in holiness.

Renewal of Baptism Vows

Reader *Romans 6:3–4, 21–13.*

A person who has been baptised recently may read.

In our baptism we died to sin, we died with Christ;
In our baptism we came alive to God, we rose with Christ.
Let us therefore renew our baptismal vows:

Baptismal vows may be renewed, using whatever form is familiar.

A sprig of rosemary may be used to sprinkle people with water.

Leader   Lord of all life and power, who through the mighty
resurrection of your Son overcame the old order of
sin and death to make all things new in him:
grant that we, being dead to sin and alive to you
in Jesus Christ, may reign with you for ever.

 A song, hymn or chant may be sung.

The Fire of Christ

*One person now lights the large Easter candle from the
fire. The people follow as this is taken to an altar or
table.*

Leader   The light of Christ.
    All   The light of Christ.

*The leader picks up a candle from the table, lights it
from the Easter Candle, and lights a neighbour's
candle with the words 'The light of Christ'. Everyone
does and says the same. Candles may remain lit until
people leave the building, and may be used again at
Sunday lunch. The lights are turned on.*

Leader   Rejoice, O earth, in shining splendour, radiant in
the brightness of your King. Christ has conquered!
Glory fills you! Darkness vanishes for ever!
    All   May the light of Christ, rising in glory, banish all
darkness from our lives.

Leader   Lift up your hearts.
    All   We lift them to the Lord.

Leader   Now you are light in the Lord. Let your light shine
before others. May the Spirit affirm you as
children of the light.
    All   Alleluia!

Song of praise.

 The Gospel reading for Sunday may be read.

 There may be free prayer.

Leader   The light of Christ in you, behind you, before you,
             till dawn breaks, and the Sun of Righteousness
             breaks forth all o'er the earth.

All   Alleluia! Amen!

Leader   Go in peace to love and serve the Lord.

All   In the name of Christ; Amen.

Easter Sunrise Service

The service takes place in the open air and begins shortly before sunrise. People gather in silence, facing east whence the sun will rise, where an Easter garden with empty tomb or a cross may be placed.

As the women who first witnessed Jesus' resurrection brought spices early in the morning to adorn His body in the garden tomb, so may we bring hearts of devotion. Some may wish to place a palm cross or a flower before the cross. Let us listen to the sounds of nature. May the birds' chorus be for us a welcome to Christ, whom the Bible calls the Morning Star, and whom the Celtic church called the Bough of Creation. Because this act of worship is in this spirit, it is sometimes felt inappropriate to have any accoutrements in worship other than the pure voice.

Leader   Sleeper, awake, rise from the dead. Light will shine upon you, Jesus Christ, Alleluia!

 Singing

Reader   *Luke 24:1–12 or John 20:11–18.*

Leader   Christ is risen!
All   He is risen indeed! Alleluia!

Leader   Rejoice, heavenly powers! Sing, choirs of angels!
Exult, all creation around God's throne.
Jesus Christ, High King of heaven, is risen!
Sound the trumpet of salvation! Alleluia!

Rejoice, O earth, in shining splendour;
Radiant in the brightness of your King!
Christ has conquered death! Glory fills you!
Darkness vanishes for ever! Alleluia!

Rejoice, O church! Exult in glory! The risen Saviour
shines upon you!
Let this place resound with joy, echoing the
mighty song of all God's people! Alleluia!

 Singing

Reader   *Matthew 28:2–6.*

Leader   Living Lord, come to us in your risen power and
make us glad with your presence.
Risen Lord, as Mary Magdalen met you by the
garden tomb on the morning of your resurrection,
so may we meet you today and every day. Speak
to us as you spoke to her. Reveal yourself to us as
our living Master. Renew our hope. Kindle our joy,
and inspire us to share the good news with others.

 Singing

*Brief words of teaching or encouragement may be
given.*

Leader   Christ was killed and rose again at the time of the
Jewish Passover festival in order to fulfil its
meaning: a crossing over. The ancient Jews crossed
over from a life of slavery to the land of promise;
Jesus crossed over from death to life. We cross over
from the slavery and death of sin to the freedom
and life of Christ. That is the meaning of our
baptism. Let us who are baptised make an act of
unity with the crucified and risen Christ, so that
this becomes the pattern of our lives.

Easter Anthem

Leader   Christ our Passover has been sacrificed for us:
So let us celebrate the feast.

All   Not with the old leaven of corruption and
wickedness: but with the unleavened
bread of sincerity and truth.

Leader   Christ once raised from the dead dies no more:
Death has no more dominion over Him.

All   In dying He died to sin once for all:
In living He lives to God.

Leader   See yourselves therefore as dead to sin:
And alive to God through Jesus Christ our Lord.

All   Christ has been raised from the dead:
The first-fruits of those who 'sleep'.

Leader   For as by man came death:
By man also has come the resurrection of the
dead.

All   For as in Adam all die:
So in Christ shall all be made alive.

Leader   We welcome the sun that lights up day:

All   We welcome the Sun of suns who dispels the
shades of sin.

Leader   The sun rises daily only because you command it;

All   Its splendour will not last, created things all
perish.

Leader   Christ the true Sun nothing can destroy;

All   The Splendour of God, he shall reign for ever!

Leader   In the light of the risen Christ, all is transformed.
Now we may look back over the past, we may look
in upon ourselves and we may look out upon the
world, and see all in a fresh light. We see people
and we pray with the 'resurrection eyes' of our
Lord Jesus. Let us have a time of prayer.

Prayers

There may be silence, free prayer, or prepared thanksgivings followed by intercessions. This may conclude with everyone saying the Lord's Prayer together. More singing may follow.

Leader Christ is risen! Alleluia!

All He is risen indeed! Alleluia!

Leader Listen to the word from God: 'Go quickly and tell the others "He is raised from the dead and is going before you".'

All May we walk in the light of your presence.

Leader The risen Christ said 'My peace I give you':
Let us give one another a sign of this gift and go in the peace of Christ.

All Thanks be to God. Alleluia!

All may give one another a sign of peace.

Breakfast may follow.

Creative Activity

Decorate a large wooden cross with flowers ready to take into the main worship later.

Ascension

For use daily between Ascension Day and Pentecost.

Leader	Christ is risen!
All	He is risen indeed. Alleluia!
Leader	Christ has ascended!
All	Our High King – He shall reign for ever. Alleluia!

There may be singing.

All Human Life with Christ is Raised

Leader	Trumpets of the earth proclaim Christ who once in earth had lain, Goes in triumph now to reign.
All	Alleluia!
Leader	He sits with God upon His throne, The Father's glory is His own; He the eternal, radiant Son.
All	Alleluia!
Leader	All human life with Him is raised, The weakest ones by heaven are praised: Now high and low on Him have gazed.
All	Alleluia!

The Word of God

Reader	*Psalm 96 or verses from the Psalm of the day.*
	For Psalm 96 all say, after verses 3, 6, 9, 13:
All	Glory and majesty surround him.

There may be singing.

Reader	Let us attend, the Word of God comes to us:
All	Thanks be to God.

Reader   Illumine our hearts, O Lord, implant in us a desire for your truth; may all that is false within us flee.

Old Testament reading.

High King

Leader	High King:
All	You are crowned with glory.

Leader	Victor in the race:
All	You call us to follow you.

Leader	High Priest:
All	You understand our every need.

Leader	Eternal Giver:
All	You shower your gifts upon every soul.

Leader	Head of the church:
All	You wish no one to be separate from your Body.

Leader	Sender:
All	You promise us your Holy Spirit.

Reader   *New Testament reading: Luke 24:50–53; Acts 1:1–11; Matthew 28:16–20; or 1 Peter 2:4–10.*

There may be a creed, silent meditation, teaching, creative activity (see below) or singing.

Prayers

Leader   High King of the universe:
Teach us to reverence you at all times;
Teach us to thank you in all things;
Teach us to look for you in all places;
Teach us to love you in all people;
Teach us to receive you in all your fullness.

High King of the universe,
In you our mortal humanity has been raised to life
in God.

*At informal gatherings a different person may read
each of the following and add to them:*

May tiny infants in the womb be raised to life in
you;
May the handicapped and ailing be raised to life
in you;
May bronzed and brave adventurers be raised to
life in you;
May thinkers and researchers be raised to life in
you;
May the battle-scarred and weary be raised to life
in you;

Any May . . . be raised to life in you.

Leader Ascended Lord, you call those who follow you to a
time of waiting, that they may be able to receive
the gifts you delight to shower on your church,
and to receive the Spirit who empowers your
church. Give us receptive hearts. Make us fertile
ground. Take away from us obstinate refusals.

There may be silence, free prayer and singing.

Blessing

Leader May the King of glory fill you with joy, keep you in
unity, give you expectant hearts, and bring you
the Strength from on high.

All Alleluia! Amen!

Creative Activities

These may precede or follow the prayers.

Ascending Prayer Balloons: *mark balloons with a prayer for one of the seven gifts of the Spirit (a different colour for each gift), fill them with gas, and go to a high place and release them.*

Building a cairn: *Read 1 Peter 2:4. Each person collects a stone which represents a prayer or a gift which they wish to offer to God. After time for reflection each person is invited to place their stone to make a cairn, with a silent or spoken word that says what the stone represents for them. When all the stones have been put in place everyone stands in a circle around the cairn and offers praise to God, ending with this prayer:*

Leader	Ascended Lord, you have made us living stones of the temple you are to build. We offer all that we are, and all that we have to you.
Leader	King of Glory:
All	Ennoble us.
Leader	King of Grace:
All	Cherish us.
Leader	King of Life:
All	Renew us.
Leader	King of Promise:
All	Surprise us.
Leader	Let us go in peace to love and serve the Lord:
All	In the name of Christ. Amen.

Pentecost

Leader   Creator Spirit, come,
                Renew the face of the earth.
                Kindling Spirit, come,
                Inflame our waiting hearts.
                Anointing Spirit, come,
                Pour forth on us anew.

There may be singing.

Leader   You led your people by a cloud:
All   May your Spirit lead us all today.
Leader   You led your people by fire at night:
All   May your Spirit lighten up our way

Psalm

Reader   *Key verses of the Psalm of the day are read.*

There may be singing.

The Word of God

Reader   Let us attend, the Word of God comes to us.
All   Thanks be to God.

Reader   May your Spirit light up your Word and illumine
                our hearts, O Lord.

Old Testament reading.

Spirit of God

Leader   Spirit of God:
All   The breath of creation is yours.

| Leader | Spirit of God: |
| All | The groans of the world are yours. |

| Leader | Spirit of God: |
| All | The wonder of communion is yours. |

| Leader | Spirit of God: |
| All | The fire of love is yours. |

| Leader | And we are filled: |
| All | And we are filled. |

| Reader | Let us attend, the Word of Christ comes to us. Hear the Word of Christ from . . . |

The New Testament reading.

| Leader | This is the Word of Christ. |
| All | Breathed by the Spirit of God. |

There may be meditation, teaching, sharing, singing, or the Creative Activity.

Creative Activity

Storytelling. One or both of the readings below are retold and illustrated in mime.

The leader then prays:

| Leader | God of the call, God of the journey, thank you for your anointings of Samson, Columba and so many other of your saints from the Day of Pentecost until now. |
| | Come to us with your anointing power. Anoint us as you will for the ministries you will. |

Here I stand, alert and open, praying that the Wild Goose[8] may come to me . . .

There may be silence, open ministry, singing in the Spirit. Different persons may pray any of the following prayers from different places as and when it feels appropriate, in which case the words to be spoken by all should be said by the person who prays.

Prayers

Reader   Holy Spirit of greatest power, come to us.
Holy Spirit, Strength-giver, may we your praises sing.
Holy Spirit, our Strong tower, may your fibre grow in us.

In the following two prayers the words to be said by all may be said by an alternative reader instead

Leader   Flame of purity:
All   Light us up.

Leader   Flame of beauty:
All   Light us up.

Leader   Flame of wisdom:
All   Light us up.

Leader   Flame of friendship:
All   Light us up.

Leader   Flame of true speech:
All   Light us up.

Leader   Flame of true seeing:
All   Light us up.

Reader   Breath of God, blow away all that is unclean:
All   Rain of God, revive our withered lives.

Reader   Wind of God, blow us to wild places as you will:
All   Breeze of God, refresh us as you desire.

Reader   River of God, flow through us and heal our land:
All   River of God, flow through us and heal our land.

Blessing

Leader   The blessing of God and the Lord be yours,
The blessing of the perfect Spirit be yours,
The blessing of the Three be pouring for you
Mildly and generously,
Hour by hour,
More and more,
And for ever.

Readings

The Holy Spirit in the life of Samson

Three brothers were to be ordained, two as
presbyters, and Samson as a deacon. As they bent
down to pray for forgiveness, Dubricius and Illtud
saw, through the open window, a dove sent from
heaven, take a fixed stand high over Samson. It
did not flutter about, as is normal with a bird, but
remained still throughout the time the ministers
went to and fro in the church. What is still more
wonderful, when the bishop raised his hand to
confirm Samson as a deacon, the dove descended
on his shoulder and continued to stay the entire
length of the service. Always that same wonderful
dove stayed silently over him, as the three looked
on, until he received the communion of the
Eucharist. . . . Samson was seen to emerge, by
daily use, renewed and bettered.

The descent of the Holy Spirit upon Columba

When Columba was living in the Hinba island,
the grace of the Holy Spirit was communicated to
him abundantly, and dwelt with him in a
wonderful manner. For three whole days and
nights, without eating or drinking, he allowed no
one to approach him, and remained confined in a

house which was filled with heavenly brightness. Yet out of that house, through the chinks of the doors and keyholes, rays of surpassing brilliance were seen to issue forth through the night. He was heard to sing certain spiritual songs also, which had never been heard before.

Summer Earth Blessing

 This service of Blessing the Earth may be held at any time (e.g. to mark the first day of spring, midsummer, or 6th August, which is the anniversary both of Christ's Transfiguration and of the bombing of Hiroshima).

As people gather in a garden, field, or a building decorated with a creation theme, there is music, quiet, rhythmic drum beats, or (if indoors) recorded sounds of sea or birds. As people arrive, representatives may bring bags of earth and place them near an earthen pot which stands in the midst of the worshippers.

Leader	The earth is the Lord's:
All	And everything in it.

Leader	Let all the people give God praise:
All	And all creation bless God's name.

 Singing or music.

Readers:

A   How precious is the soil the Lord has made. It is rich and fertile; a single seed planted in her will bring forth a hundred seeds.

B   How beautiful is the soil the Lord has made. Frail seeds blown by gentle winds become garlands of colour flowering in crevice and cranny.

C   How mysterious is the soil the Lord has made. Its deeps bring forth minerals which bring buildings, energy and ornament to our lives.

D   How fruitful is the soil the Lord has made. It brings
     forth crops of wheat and wood, of fruits and nuts,
     of roots and berries.

E   How hospitable is the soil the Lord has made. Can
     the sheep and cows eat grass without the soil?
     Even the birds who soar above the highest
     mountain must return to earth to find food. The
     earth provides a bed for the ocean, and a floor for
     humankind.

F   How like a mother is the soil the Lord has made. It
     contains us and feeds us, it warms us and sustains
     us.

All   Lord bless our land and your children who live
     by it.

Reader   *Psalm 96 or Psalm 148.*

Praise for the Plants

*The leader displays a list of plants that grow in the
locality. Some participants may be asked to bring a
plant, or to add to the list.*

Leader   Let us each raise a hand of praise towards the sky.
     For —— (*name the plant*).

All   We praise you, generous Giver.

Leader   Now let us repeat that, but this time each person
     names a plant of their choice, all together:

All   For —— (*name of plant*) we praise you, generous
     Giver.

Leader   High King of the universe, thank you for these
     plants your earth gives to us, and for all the
     blessings of life you shower upon us. In your
     goodness we ask you to let the soil bring forth
     abundance of life, and to renew the joy of all your
     children on earth.

A reading

from the Old Testament.

Reader   *One of these passages or another passage may be read: Leviticus 25:1–12; Proverbs 30:21–33; Isaiah 24:1–13.*

There may be a talk, followed by meditative singing.

Sorrow and Penitence

Leader   Land in the Bible is seen as God's gift to His people. They only have what they need. They show their gratitude by not selling it, mortgaging it, or letting it be eroded. They do not misuse it, they respect it, give it rest, and steward it for future generations. But when people violate God's moral laws, then everything, including the very soil, is spoiled. God calls us to repent for the hardness of heart of ourselves and of our fellows.

Leader   For ugly buildings that violate the shape of the land and the human soul's need for beauty.

Leader   For the rain forests gone, and the deserts caused by human destruction.

Leader   For polluted seas, dirty streets, and litter:
All   We grieve with you, O Lord.

Leader   For demanding such variety of food and drink that we are not content to have things in season:
All   We grieve with you, O Lord.

Leader   For not being content to savour the simple gifts of creation:
All   We grieve with you, O Lord.

A reading

from the New Testament.

Reader   *Mark 9: 2–10 (for 6th August) or Matthew 21:33–41.*

Leader   Dear Creator, teach us to care for your earth, and
be good stewards of all that is in it. May our eyes
be open to see your hand in nature;
May our hands be open to cherish your gifts in the
material things around;
May we learn how to live in harmony with your
laws.

The Blessing of the Earth

*The representatives of different parts of the
neighbourhood place the earth they have brought in
an earthen pot. The leader lays his/her hand on the
earth:*

Leader   Lord, bless this, the soil on which we live, and
work and make community. In your mercy may it
bring forth goodness to nourish and renew the
whole community who shares it.

You made the earth and through the long ages
planted it with every kind of plant; you made
animals to crawl and to run upon it, birds to fly
over it, and fish to swim around it. When all was
prepared, you formed humankind from the soil.
You breathed your life into them.

May we never forget that we are mortal creatures;
from earth we come, to earth we go. We did not
make ourselves. Indeed, we and the earth itself
need to be redeemed through the Saviour who
restored unity between earth and heaven. In the
name of the One who came from heaven yet was
born of earth, let us each bless the earth.

In a moment of recollection each person becomes
tuned to their surroundings, chooses a patch of ground
or a living thing, and lays a hand of blessing upon it,
praying silently. A song may be sung.

If there is Holy Communion these words are said:

Leader   Blessed are you, King of all the universe, for these
         gifts of bread and wine which earth has given and
         human hands have made. May they become for
         us the food and drink of eternal life.
All   Bless the King of all the earth.

If there is Holy Communion the leader repeats the
words of Christ instituting the Lord's Supper . . .

Leader   When the Saviour of this globe was stretched out
         on the Tree of death, the elements erupted and the
         earth gave up its dead. His blood, spilled on the
         soil, transfigured earth and heaven.
         May His body and blood change us and
         transfigure this earth.
         Transfigure this earth:
All   May your kingdom come on it.

Leader   Transfigure this earth:
All   May flowers bloom on it.

Leader   Transfigure this earth:
All   May peace reign on it.

Leader   Transfigure this earth:
All   May people and animals be friends on it.

Leader   Transfigure this earth:
All   May our bodies be changed into bodies of
         resurrection.

Those who wish are given the bread and wine with
words such as 'The body of Christ restore harmony to
you and yours'. The laying on of hands silently (unless

a specific request is made) for the restoration of harmony within and without is offered in different places. There may be quiet singing during this ministry. If appropriate, those who are not receiving ministry may leave after the following prayers.

 Prayers

All   We will cherish the digging.
We will cherish the buying.
We will cherish the cooking.
We will cherish the eating.
We will cherish the plants.
We will cherish the birds.
We will cherish the travelling.
We will cherish the love-making.

Any   We will cherish the . . .

 Singing

Blessing

Leader   Bless to us, O God,
The moon that is above us,
The earth that is beneath us,
Your friends who are around us,
Your image deep within us.

Let us go in peace to cherish the Lord in all things on earth.

All   In the name of Christ. Amen.

harvests

---

*Lammas is the season of the various harvests. In Celtic
tradition this season begins on 1st August. Later
comes the harvest of the hedges – fruits and berries.
It ends by 1st November with the gathering in of the
nuts. Activities associated with food and welfare such
as spinning, weaving, and shoe-making were part of
the celebrations which included mime and dance.
So today it is important that we include in our
celebrations all the things that make our common life
productive.*

Leader   The earth is the Lord's and everything in it. Whose
            is the earth?

All   The earth is the Lord's.

There may be singing.

An Iona Benedicite

After each line everyone responds (R):

All   Praise him and magnify him for ever.

Leader   O angels of the Lord, bless the Lord. (R)
            O saints of these parts, bless the Lord. (R)
            O servants of Christ who here sang God's praises,
            bless the Lord. (R)
            O souls of the faithful who rest in Jesus, bless the
            Lord. (R)
            O kindly folk of this place, bless the Lord. (R)
            O sheep and horned cattle, O lambs that gambol
            on the green, bless the Lord. (R)

O fish that glisten in the waters, bless the Lord. (R)
O rooks that caw from the sycamores, O buzzards
that float on the wind currents, bless the Lord. (R)
O gulls that fill the beaches with your clamour, O
terns and gannets that dive headlong for your
prey, O dunlins that wheel in unison over the
waves, bless the Lord. (R)
O larks that carol in the heavens, O blackbirds
that pipe at the dawning, O pipits and wheatears,
O warblers and wrens that make the fields joyful
with song; O bees that love the heather, bless the
Lord. (R)
O flowers that gem the earth with colour, O golden
flags that deck the beds with glory, bless the Lord.
(R)
O piled rocks, fashioned by Nature's might
through myriad ages, O majestic peaks, O white
sands and emerald shallows, O blue and purple
deeps of ocean, O winds and cloud, bless the Lord.
(R)
O all works of the Lord, bless the Lord. (R)

 The Word of God

Reader   *Psalm 65 or verses from another Psalm.*

 There may be singing.

Reader   *Leviticus 23:37–44 or another reading from the Old
Testament.*

A Confession

Leader   Father, the good things of your earth shout out
          your praise; forgive us that our lives so seldom
          speak of gratitude.
          Father, have mercy.
   All   Father, have mercy.

Leader	Lord, these good things are denied to people in other parts of your earth; forgive us for pollution, neglect, and greed.
	Lord, have mercy.
All	Lord, have mercy.

Leader	Spirit, these good things would not be here unless their seeds of life had first laid still in the rhythms of winter's soil; forgive us for trying to be what we are not and for resisting your rhythms.
	Spirit, have mercy.
All	Spirit, have mercy.

Reader	*Matthew 6:25–34 or another reading from the New Testament.*

Silent meditation, teaching, sharing or creative activity.

 Creative Activities

1. Beforehand, create a display of harvest produce that includes anything that makes for human well-being.
2. Mime one or both of the Bible readings.
3. Each person is invited to think of an equivalent in their life of the little cow, and to write a prayer for it in similar fashion. Then do the same with the Butter Prayer, praying for something you, or others, greatly need.
4. Instead of the Iona Benedicite, together create a Benedicite that reflects your neighbourhood. Use this before the blessing.
5. Afterwards, make one or more huts out of twigs, cardboard or straw, with an open roof, draw up a rota of people who will stay in it for at least an hour (maybe through the night). While doing their rota, people write down their reflections and bring them to the next occasion of corporate worship.

There may be singing.

Prayers

Bless my Cow

Leader   Bless, O God, my little cow,
Bless, O God, my desire;
Bless our partnership
And the milking of my hands, O God.
Bless, O God, each teat,
Bless, O God, each finger,
Bless each drop
That goes into my pitcher.

Group   *(if any)* Bless my . . .

The Butter Prayer

Leader   You who put beam in moon and sun,
You who put food in ear and herd,
You who put fish in stream and sea,
Send the butter up in time.

Come, you rich lumps, come!
Come, you rich lumps, come!
Come, you rich lumps, masses large,
Come, you rich lumps, come!

Group   *(if any)* You . . .
Come . . .

Group   *(if any) The Local Benedicite.*

Blessing

Leader   Bless to us, O God,
The moon that is above us,
The earth that is beneath us,
All creatures who are around us,
Your image deep within us.

ḣealinꞬ ṫhe Lanꝺ

*Healing the land brings the church's healing ministry
to bear on the environment and on communal memory.
Any or all of these Acts of Prayer may be used.*

Healing through Rest

Reader   *Genesis 2:1–3; Exodus 23:10–12.*

Meditation

Leader   The need for rest was built into creation (*Genesis
2:1–3*). Under the guidelines God gave the people
of Israel, the land was to be given a rest every
seventh year. This was to be echoed in a weekly
cycle (*Exodus 23:10–12*). There was a law of limited
cropping – 'enough is enough'. In the New
Testament a grasping attitude is equally clearly
exposed and condemned. Jesus said 'Out of a
person's heart comes . . . ruthless greed' (*Mark
17:21*).

So the people were called to strive for the ideal of
shalom – the harmony of a caring community
that is aware that every aspect of human life and
of the earth is related to God.

Creative Activity

*Make a Rule of Life for yourself which makes practical
the requirement of Rest in everyday life. Return in ten
minutes and talk it through with one person, and vice
versa (five minutes each).*

Prayer

*Each person repeats this prayer, with rhythmic
breathing, for at least five minutes.*

Rest in the Lord *(breathing in)*.
Earth and all that breathes *(breathing out)*.

*The next two Acts of Prayer focus on the healing of
group memory. We are all shaped by group memory
and carry it within us. Our group memories may be
family, tribal, church, city or national. Some of these
group memories may carry such deep wounds they
severely damage the present. Before meaningful acts of
healing can take place, representative people need to
engage in a process of discernment that involves
'knowing the story', and sensing the root attitudes
requiring healing that the story reveals.*

*Healing the land involves 'representational
confession'. As we pray we confess as our own the past
sins of our group, even if we were not involved at the
time the action took place. Our models for doing this
are Jesus, who took upon himself the sins of every
group, and biblical characters such as Nehemiah, who
took upon themselves the sins of their nation.*

Healing through Repentance

There may be informal singing and worship.

Reader   *Genesis 3:1–19.*

Meditation

Leader   The garden (the creation) was filled with an
                 abundance of good things for the blessing of
                 human beings (*verse 2; see also 2:9*). Yet God

required them to accept limitation. There was one tree they were not to eat, since they were not designed for infinite consumption. The law of 'enough is enough' was built into the universe (*verse 3*). The sin of the first human being brings a curse on the soil (*verse 17*). Negative human behaviour and attitudes have an effect on the things of the earth.

Reader   *Exodus 20:5.*

Meditation

Leader   This is part of the Ten Commandments. Moses' people were told not to make objects of worship out of things of the earth. If they did, the sins of the parents would afflict three or four following generations. We see that a sin committed in the past can have a chain reaction.

Reader   *Proverbs 30:21–23.*

Meditation – Four Vibrations of Violence

Leader   The message is that four things create such disease that the earth itself is affected. There is a connection between human behaviour and the earth. The earth cannot tolerate these four types of people:
1. Usurpers, i.e. pushy people who unnaturally break into the natural rhythms of human life (*verse 21*). These people are not following a calling, they are trying to be what they are not. Betray people, and you betray the land.
2. Layabouts who behave as if the world owes them a living; people with a surfeit of things they can't handle appropriately; parasites who take all but give nothing (*verse 22*). Steal from people, and you steal from the land.

3. Brides who hate their bridegroom. A relationship designed for loving, entered into by a hard and hate-filled person (*verse 23*). Hate people, and you hate the land.

4. Employees of a woman who have sex with her husband. A sexual appetite (or any other appetite) takes over a person and drives out respect for human relationships. Rape people, and you rape the land.

Creative Activity

Write on card the four sentences which follow and pin these to your clothing:
Betray people, and you betray the land.
Steal from people, and you steal from the land.
Hate people, and you hate the land.
Rape people, and you rape the land.

Now each person writes a list on a separate piece of paper of one or more sins that bring sorrow to the creation.

Leader   Listen to this reading from Blathmac of creation's sorrow for our sins that crucified Christ:

Reader   The sun concealed its proper light; it lamented its Lord. A swift cloud went across the blue sky, the great stormy sea roared. The whole world became dark, great trembling came upon the earth; at the noble death of Jesus great rocks burst open. . . . A fierce stream of blood boiled until the bark of every tree was red. . . . It would have been fitting for God's elements – the fair sea, the blue sky, the earth – to have changed their appearance, lamenting their calamity. The body of Christ exposed to the spear thrust demanded harsh lamentation – that they should have mourned more grievously the Man by whom they were created.

Silence.

Bring the pieces of paper to the leader and read out the sins that bring sorrow to the creation.

The leader, or any who wish, say prayers of penitence.

Leader   Have mercy on us Lord, have mercy. Forgive us for these sins, through the poured-out blood of the Saviour of the world.

All   Amen.

Healing through Resurrection

Reader   *1 Corinthians 15:28; 1 Corinthians 19:12.*

Meditation

Leader   Jesus' resurrection was a physical as well as a spiritual resurrection. It involved a healing pattern that affected matter, including bones. God wants us to treat life as an organic whole. Through his resurrection Jesus was made Lord over all creation, and all enemies are now under His feet. This includes the enemy of the original curse upon the land resulting from Adam's sin. The resurrection touches all times, places and elements. Christians are to share Jesus' rule which extends not only to believers but to the whole universe. We share this rule with the one whom 'the wind and the waves obey' not by our own power but as channels of the Spirit. Thus the gifts which were meant for humans from the beginning of creation, but were lost, such as the power to bless, were restored through the resurrection of Jesus. Healing is not only repairing; it is a new creation.

Singing

People are asked beforehand to each bring quite a large stone from the locality. Each one now holds their stone, which represents for them some sin from the communal memory.

Leader We name the dark practices, the selfish deeds, the shame or neglect which we believe this place has imbibed.

Each person names the sin which their stone represents and places it in a heap in the midst of the gathering. The leader brings water from a baptistry, font, well or tap and blesses it. The leader then pours water over these stones with words such as these:

Leader We repent of these, and of sins of this place that are unknown to us.
In the name of the holy and almighty God, may the cleansing power of the Creator, the cleansing blood of the Saviour, and the cleansing water of the Spirit wash over the sins of time, the deeds of shame, the thoughts that destroy . . .

Now a cross is placed in the ground amid the stones.

Leader We plant Christ's Cross in this ground.
In Christ's name we say: May this land be set free from the power of the past to control the present; may this place be set free from the bitterness of memories. In this place may healing take place and wholeness be restored; may this be heavenly land.

Reader When Jesus rode into the city on a donkey, and the authorities wanted the disciples to cease their acclaim, Jesus said: 'If they were to keep quiet the very stones themselves will start shouting' *(based on Luke 19:40).*

Leader	Let us each pick up a stone, for now these are to become stones of blessing. May the land these stones represent be set free to be one with God, to be free as the wide skies above, free as the wind of God's Spirit, free to be fruitful, free for all things good to flourish, free for all that is meant to be. To the glory and praise of heaven's King, the God and Lord of all.
All	Amen.

People may walk around holding their stones of blessing, speaking out blessings or silently communing. This may be followed by informal worship or refreshments.

A Whitby Act of Healing

A 'Healing the Land' service may take place on an anniversary of a significant local or national event, or at a place where historic change took place which still affects us. The following example may be used at Whitby, or may be used as a model to be adapted in other places. The Community of Aidan and Hilda encourage prayer for the healing of the land on St Hilda's Day, 17th November.

At Whitby Abbey, where Hilda welcomed Roman and Celtic delegates to a church synod in 664, church regulations were imposed on the indigenous Celtic church in a way which crushed its life and witness.Whatever the rights and wrongs of the regulations themselves, the manner of their imposition ruptured the basis of the church as a fellowship of mutual trust and love.

A representative of a church regulated from Canterbury, a representative of a church regulated from Rome, and a representative of independent, indigenous churches should take part.

Lament

Each representative kneels on the Whitby earth before a bare cross and says in turn these or similar words:

Rep O Lord we lament, how we lament –
The loss in the church of integrity, humility and patience;
The crushing of spontaneity;
The caging of the Wild Goose;
The bruising of the crushed reeds;
The arrogance of the intellect;
The pride of empire-building.

Everyone present repeats these words together.

Each representative says in turn:

I accept our share of responsibility for these sins. I seek to shed these sins on behalf of myself and my church. Have mercy upon us and forgive us.

The representative now kisses the earth.

I embrace this earth and say on behalf of myself and my church: Be reconciled with the earth, and with all the people who have followed Christ on this earth; those in heaven and those who live today.

Silence.

Rekindling and Blessing

A religious sister or other representative of the churches of Whitby says:

In the spirit of Hilda, we pray, Lord, for a re-kindling of –

Each representative says in turn:

Rep Holy callings.

Rep Contemplative prayer.

Rep Spiritual warfare.

Rep Signs and wonders.

Rep The adventure of divine obedience.

Rep Cherishing the poor and weak.

Rep Delight in local colour and character.

Rep The moving with the flow of all that is good in the hearts of the people.

Rep Rootedness in the soil.

Rep Dependence upon your Spirit.

Creative Activities

Others present may wish to kiss the sweet earth of Whitby and bless it and call for a re-kindling in our church and our land of these or other blessings which they speak out, or carry written on flags, prayer sticks or paper flowers as they walk around the grounds. Some may wish to write out a covenant with God singly or as a group which incorporates the vision of the healing of a split land and a split people of God. They then read these out in the presence of other groups, and send them to places such as Canterbury and Rome.

There may be singing.

Representatives from different traditions may now embrace one another with words such as these:

Rep The peace of the Lord be with you. I seek your forgiveness for all wrong attitudes of the past, and pray that in the place of hostility, love may grow; that in the place of division, wholeness may grow; that we may walk the pilgrimage of trust on earth no longer as strangers but as pilgrims together.

Everyone joins hands.

All   We swear by peace and love to stand
Heart to heart and hand in hand;
Mark, O Spirit, and hear us now,
Confirming this our Sacred Vow

There may be singing and sharing of refreshments.

Prayer Walks

Prayer walks can take place any time, anywhere. They can range from a few friends who are inspired to do an impromptu prayer walk incognito, to a major occasion that involves the whole Body of Christ in an area, with carefully planned route, music, amplification etc.

Blessing

An ancient Christian custom is to bless the life and work of an area. In agricultural areas people may walk with tractors, stop where there are different crops and ask blessing on the seeds that have been planted. In industrial areas people may walk with an open top bus or a car trailer, blessing different kinds of commerce, industry or leisure activity. Here is an example of an ancient prayer of blessing, which can be adapted to the situation:

> O Monarch of the Tree of Life,
> May the blossoms bring forth the sweetest fruit,
> May the birds sing out the highest praise,
> May your Spirit's gentle breath cover all.

Circling

Celtic Christians carried on the ancient custom of circling places. This is called The Caim. Everyone may hold hands and walk around a building or place. If this is not practical, everyone may point their index finger towards an area, and turn round in a complete circle. Here is an example of a Caim Prayer:

Circle this place, Lord
Keep evil out, keep good within
Keep greed without, keep care within
Keep addiction out, keep faith within
Keep prejudice out, keep respect within
Keep injustice out, keep truth within
Keep disease without, keep wholeness within.

'Glastonbury' Prayer Walks

Certain places accrue particular dynamics, through natural force fields, historical association or current use, for good or ill. These make obvious focal points for prayer walks. The following prayer walk is based on Glastonbury, which is known in southern Britain as a place that cradles new spirituality.

It can be adapted and used as a model for other places. Penitence should be made in a place that speaks of dominance; prayer for cleansing may be said in a place associated with fire or cleansing. A high place or building or the Town Hall may be used to pray for atonement. A place of resource for the neighbourhood such as a park, power station or reservoir may be used to pray for God's refreshing. Prayer for the transforming of sin and suffering may take place at a crematorium, a hospital or at a morally shady area. Praise should flow from local churches.

From Glastonbury Abbey's St Patrick's Chapel – Penitence

Scripture meditation: Luke 18:9–14.

St Patrick taught all Christians to frequently pray 'Lord, have mercy upon us'.

Confess and repent on behalf of all Christians for the things that have caused offence to others in the Christian history of the area. For all that has

> belittled others;
> estranged others;

> crushed others;
> neglected others;
> excluded others.

Repeat the Jesus Prayer ('Lord Jesus Christ, have mercy upon me a sinner') with rhythmic breathing as you walk around the abbey or other churches and places.

From the Bridget Chapel – cleansing fire

Scripture meditation: Luke 3:16, 17.

In this all-faiths chapel for silent prayer, which is part of The Glastonbury Experience complex, silently use the worship resources for St Brigid's Day. The Christian Saint Brigid of Kildare (who is reputed to have stayed at Glastonbury) replaced the pagan flame in the Oak Grove at Kildare with a flame that was kept alight for 1,000 years. Take a candle to light and leave in the chapel, or a covered lantern to take out with you. Bring to God all the things that need to be burned out and purified – wrong attitudes, beliefs, practices.

Then go throughout the town praying that the cleansing fire will come to anything you see which is impure.

From the Tor – Atonement

Scripture meditation: Colossians 1:15–22.

Walk to the top of the Tor with a crucifix or cross. (A crucifix underlines the fact that the Christian God is not, as pagans believe, merely a God of the sky; God has come among us in human flesh.) Meditate on the cross as the place of atonement (at-one-ment) between:

> heaven and earth;
> male and female;
> a groaning creation and the Creator;
> divided families, groups, nations;
> the land and the people;
> the past and the present.

Pray for reconciliation and healing as you walk back around the town with the crucifix or cross.

From the Chalice Well – the living waters

Scripture meditation: John 4:13–15.

Meditate on the life-giving waters that come from the heart of God for healing, peace, renewal. Reflect on your baptism. Invite God's Holy Spirit to pour out afresh upon you these gifts of healing, peace, renewal. As you wander around the garden ask the renewing Spirit to bring these gifts to others. Some may wish to take a container of water to bless, and to sprinkle water from this with a sprig at different streets and places.

From the Glastonbury Thorn – the fruits of the Spirit

Scripture meditation: Galatians 5:22, 23.

A thorn at Weary-all Hill is near the spot where the original thorn is reputed to have been planted by Joseph of Arimathea. Other thorns grow in the Abbey grounds and elsewhere. These all flower twice in one year.

Pray that out of the thorny situations that exist, the nine fruits of the Spirit may flower. These are: love, joy, peace, patience, kindness, goodness, faithfulness, humility and self-control. With groups, each person may take one fruit (perhaps carrying an intercession stick with a colour that represents that fruit), and prayer walk into the highways and byways of the area.

In churches, chapels and gathering places – praise.

Scripture meditation: Isaiah 51:3.

'Put on the garments of praise, O Jerusalem.' Let music and singing, contemplation and praise through creative arts flow in all these places.

Praying with the Celtic Saints

St Fursey

16th January

Leader   ✠ In the Name of God the All-seeing;
In the Name of Heaven's Son;
In the name of the eagle-eyed Spirit;
In the name of the Three-In-One.

God of the journey, whose holy scholar Fursey,
impelled by the visions you entrusted to him, gave
his life as a pilgrim for love of you, spare us your
anger, and help us to heed and speed your word,
through Jesus Christ our Lord.

All   Amen.

A Vision of Fursey

Leader   The saints shall advance from one virtue to
another:

All   The God of gods shall be seen among us.

Leader   We shall be changed from glory to glory:
All   The God of gods shall be seen among us.

Leader   The fire of God shall purge the wastelands:
All   The God of gods shall be seen among us.

Leader   Destroyers and demons will have to flee:
All   The God of gods shall be seen among us.

Leader   The kingdoms of this world shall become the
kingdoms of our God:

All   The God of gods shall be seen among us.

    𝄞   *There may be singing.*

Penitence for the Four Sins

Leader   From all that is false and flirts with evil:
    All   Good Lord, deliver us. *(pause)*

Leader   From the love of riches and from greed and envy:
    All   Good Lord, deliver us. *(pause)*

Leader   From insensitive words and from discord and strife:
    All   Good Lord, deliver us. *(pause)*

Leader   From manipulation and abuse of others:
    All   Good Lord, deliver us. *(pause)*

The Word of God

Any or all of these passages may be read.

Reader   *Psalm 48.*

Reader   *Job 33:15–30.*

A meditation, such as the reading of 'The Dream of the Rood' or silence.

Reader   *Revelation 20:11–21:4.*

At a Communion service Matthew 13:36–43 may be read.

The Life of Fursey

A reading from the Life of Fursey (below); teaching or meditation on the visions (recorded by Bede) of the Life of Fursey.

Singing

Prayers

Leader   Watching and praying, we draw near to you, High King of the universe. We glimpse your awesome presence in the gleaming pools, in the gentle coves, in storm and thunder, and in the stillness of the night. Reveal to us the mysteries of heaven; rebuke us for our wretched ways, and bring us to the place of holiness through your Son, the Prince of peace, Jesus Christ our Saviour and Lord.

All Amen.

Leader Lord, make us ready to be pilgrims for love of you, to go wherever you open the doors.

Leader Open the doors of devotion to your word;
Open the doors of devotion to prayer and vigil;
Open the doors of devotion to the eternal mysteries;
Open the doors of devotion to sorrow and restitution.
Open the doors of devotion to good deeds;
Open the doors of devotion to truth and justice.

Any *Topics for prayer are welcome using the introduction 'Open the doors of . . .'*

Leader Good and gracious God, grant us a glimpse of your glory.
Deliver us from the darkness of night.
Give us a share with your saints in light
That we too may live to your glory, Father, Son and Holy Spirit.

 There may be singing.

Leader May the angels guard you along the road.
May heaven's praises be in you where'ere your abode.
May the Three-fold Glory your life enfold.

All Amen.

THE LIFE OF FURSEY

In AD 633 the Irish monk Fursey arrived in East Anglia to convert to Christianity the pagan Angles, who 200 years before had slaughtered or driven out the native British, and with them, the Christian faith. Fursey's companions included his brothers, Foillan and Ultan, and two priests, Gobban and Dicull. They were welcomed by King Sigebert, who had become a Christian in Gaul whence he fled for his life. On becoming king of the Angles in 631 Sigebert brought with him Bishop Felix of Burgundy, who had begun to evangelise the kingdom from his southern base at Dunwich. Sigebert gave Fursey a more northern base, at Burgh Castle, the site of the last fort the Romans built before they left Britain; and he encouraged him to spread his deep, direct experience of God that was so typical of the Celtic Christians.

Fursey was born of noble Irish blood about 597 in Connaught, near Lough Corrib, and it was said that he was baptised by St Brendan. From childhood he devoured the Scriptures, and was sent to study under Abbot Meldan on the Island of Inisquin. He spent ten years preaching the Good News of Christ, attracted large crowds, and during this time he founded a monastery at Killfursa (now named Killarsagh). In time, he felt God was calling him to a mission elsewhere, and he and a team prepared themselves on a small island off the west coast. He had probably heard that the King of the Angles had been asking for missionaries. At any rate, they set sail, and whether by design or by divine winds, they arrived in East Anglia.

In East Anglia Fursey converted many unbelievers to Christ by his holy example and by his eloquence. It seems likely they often crossed the estuary near Great Yarmouth in a coracle, to bring the Gospel to much of what is now Norfolk. During this time he became ill and received a series of powerful visions of heaven and judgment. Bede records the vision of Fursey looking down upon earth and seeing four fires; an angel told him that in time they would consume the whole world. The fires were called Falsehood, Covetousness, Discord, and

Cruelty. Ever afterwards he confronted people with the choice between life or death with an intensity that made him sweat. Fursey's visions were written down and collected. They heralded a type of literature that became widely popular in the Middle Ages; these influenced and reached their climax in Dante's 'Divine Comedy'.

Sigebert resigned as king, entered a monastery, but was later killed in battle against the pagan king of Mercia. The new regent King, Anna, was a devout Christian, and his three daughters each pursued a religious life in different parts of the kingdom. Anna greatly extended the Burgh Castle monastery, and the grip of paganism loosened its hold on his kingdom. Soon Fursey's brother, Ultan, followed a call to become an anchorite in Fenland. After ten years as abbot, Fursey joined Ultan for a year, and appointed his other brother as abbot at Burgh Castle. Fursey shared Ultan's life of prayer and austerity, supporting himself by manual labour.

About 644 Fursey, ever the pilgrim, and perhaps sensing the impending devastation by the pagan Penda, responded to the opening of a door in France. He arrived in Mezerolle just after the only son of its ruler, Duke Hayman, had died. Fursey restored him to life. Hayman implored him to stay in vain. Near Paris, King Clovis II and his beautiful English wife Bathild welcomed Fursey, and the Chief Minister Earconwald gave him land at Lagney, by the river Marne, on which to build a monastery to serve the district in Christ's name. After this was well established Fursey set out to visit his brothers in East Anglia, but he became ill at Mezerolles and died in a monastery of Irish monks in 649 or 650.

After Fursey's death, Burgh Castle, amongst other monasteries was destroyed (it was probably rebuilt and survived to the ninth century). Fursey's two brothers escaped to Peronne, but they were murdered while engaged in Christian service.

Earconwald secured the saint's body for the chapel he was building near Peronne Abbey, a monastery which followed the teachings of St Patrick. Four years later the body was still free of corruption. Miracles occurred at the shrine. Irish and other pilgrims flocked to the abbey, which became a great pilgrimage centre of St Fursey, and a hostel for pilgrims on their way to Rome or the Holy Land. Devotion to him flourished throughout Picardy.

Places to visit

England: Burgh Castle, near Great Yarmouth. Remains of the Celtic community were found in the NE corner of the Roman Fort; the church has a window of Fursey in Celtic tonsure, drawn from a medieval manuscript with perhaps his actual features; the churchyard's Fursey memorial cross is inscribed in Latin: 'Holy Fursey, Teacher, Holy Fursey, Apostle'.

France: Peronne: St John the Baptist Church contains Fursey's skull. Lagney: Chapel of Fursey.

Ireland: Inisquin; Killarsagh (Killfursa).

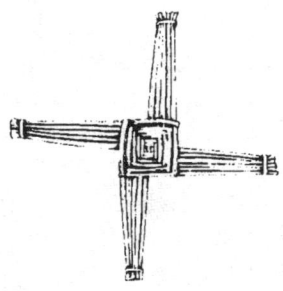

St Brigid

1st February

This falls on the day of Imbolc, the pre-Christian Celtic season that marks the coming of the light of Spring after the dark days of winter. On St Brigid's Day each year a cross is blessed and placed in homes and outhouses as an extended prayer to ward off the dark powers of evil and hunger. This custom stems from the account of how Brigid nursed and witnessed to a pagan chief. To help make the Gospel clear to him she made a cross from the rush matting, and he subsequently became a Christian. Those who observe this custom may take rush crosses to their home after this service and use prayers of blessing for a home (see notes).

A Mid-wife of the Faith

These opening words may be spoken by a group, otherwise:

All   The ever excellent woman,
The brilliant, sparkling flame;
The bird alert on the cliff-edge,
The healer of sick and lame.
She never was half-hearted
About the love of God;
She never craved for profit
But loved her bounteous Lord.
A mid-wife of the Faith was she,
A farm worker and nun,
All glory gave she to her Friend.
And we praise the Three-in-One.

Leader   Generous Lord, you inspired in Saint Brigid such wholehearted dedication to your work that she is known as Mary of the Gael; may we so follow her example that we, too, may bear much fruit in your kingdom.

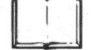

The Word of God

Reader   *Psalm 128.*

'Praise God from whom all blessings flow' or another song of praise may be sung.

Reader   *Joel 2:21–27.*

'Praise God from whom all blessings flow' or another song of praise may be sung again.

Reader   *Luke 5:1–11.*

The Life of Brigid

There is a reading from The Life of Brigid (below). This may be followed by teaching, sharing or Creative Activity.

Creative Activity

Either make four visual prayer corners which each illustrate one of these themes of Brigid's life: hospitality; healing; witness; creativity. Or make Brigid crosses out of rushes to take to homes afterwards.

Singing

Prayers

If possible these should be accompanied by sign language or illustrative movements.

Leader	You who put beam in moon and sun,
	You who put food in ear and herd,
	You who put fish in stream and sea,
	Send your blessing up to me.
	Bring forth the warmth, the tears, the laughter
	from our repressed and frozen ground.
	Bring forth loving, healing, forgiving, to our
	fretting, festering wound.
	Bring in light and truth and dancing after dark
	and frigid years.
	Bring in singing, sowing, serving, in place of
	stagnant, stubborn fears.
	Bring in scripting, painting, worship, after
	doubting, shrunken prayers.

Reader	Mary's Son, my friend, come and bless the kitchen.
	May we have fullness through you.

Reader	Mary's Son, my friend, come and bless the work.
	May we have fullness through you.

Reader	Mary's Son, my friend, come and bless the soil.
	May we have fullness through you.

Any	Mary's Son, my friend, come and bless the . . .
	May . . . have fullness through you.

Any	*When Brigid was made a nun she took as her special text Jesus' words 'Blest are those who show mercy'. In groups or together, pray for people who are in particular need of God's mercy.*

 There may be singing.

Brigid crosses may be distributed.

| Leader | As we go to our homes we pray that they, like Brigid's, may be places of hospitality and holiness, with the Cross of our Saviour Jesus Christ at their heart. |

Blessing

| Leader | May the calm that was Brigid's pinion you;
May the good that was Brigid's preserve you;
May the vitality that was Brigid's power you;
In the name of God the ever-fruitful Three. |

THE LIFE OF BRIGID OF KILDARE

The historical Brigid, a contemporary of Patrick, was the spiritual midwife who helped bring to birth Christian Ireland. She is 'the most celebrated Irish woman of all time' (Alice Curtayne), and a potent Christian symbol of womanhood. When she was on her way to a synod at Leinster, the Bishop said 'I see Mary coming', and she became known as 'the Mary of the Gael', that is, 'of the people'. Through her compassion, energy, and healing powers everything she set her hand to used to increase. Her large monastery at Kildare, in the central plain of Ireland, replaced the influence of pagan kings.

Brigid was born about AD 455, the daughter of Leinster's pagan King Dubtach and his bondswoman, Broicsech, who was a Christian. After Brigid was conceived two Bishops from Scotland prophesied over her mother. Dubtach's infertile, jealous wife forced him to sell Broicsech as a slave to a druid priest.

Brigid used to throw up the food provided by the priest, so a good local woman was allowed to feed her from her own stock. Brigid wanted to be holy and from her earliest days she rejected anything that was not wholesome. She grew strong and bold, and liberally fed the sheep, the birds and the poor. She then returned to her father's house, where she exasperated Dubtach by her habit of giving away his food and goods. She constantly took the initiative. Once when she was travelling with her father her attendant was taken ill. She fetched water from a well, prayed over it, and gave it to him to drink; it tasted like ale and he recovered.

Brigid's mother continued as a hard-working slave, and Brigid often returned to help her. A song she sang as she churned the butter for her mother and their many visitors is recorded in *Lives of the Saints from the Book of Lismore:* 'Mary's Son, my friend, come to bless this kitchen. May we have fullness through you.' Through Brigid the Lord multiplied the butter as he once multiplied loaves and fishes. Eventually this faith-filled way of life won the heart of the druid, who became a Christian, and he gave Brigid's mother her freedom.

Dubtach, despairing of Brigid's generosity with his goods, arranged a marriage of his beautiful daughter to a member of a noble family. She refused; so Dubtach allowed her to become a nun and gave her a dowry. When Brigid took the veil an old bishop was so awe-struck by the holy fire he saw above her, that he unintentionally read the words of the consecration of a bishop over her. He told a colleague who objected: 'I have no power in this matter; this dignity has been given by God to Brigid.'

Brigid resolved to establish a community where women could work and pray together. The ruler in Kildare refused her request for a grant of land, but relented when she said she would accept a plot of land the size of her cloak. Once she had a foothold, however, the area of land never seemed to stop growing. The church was built in a place that had been set aside for pagan worship, where a sacred flame was always kept alight. So the nuns, too, kept a fire of resurrection burning outside the church, night and day, and this was not extinguished for a thousand years.

Brigid needed priests to perform the sacraments, so she chose Bishop Conleath to govern with her, but there was no doubt who was in charge! Through Conleath there came monks and many skilled craftsmen, and a double monastery of men and women was established under her leadership. Sick people came to the monastery and were healed, lepers were given barrels full of apples, bishops, kings, and saints, such as Finnian before he set up his monastery at Clonard, came for advice.

The monastery brewed ale for the churches around and, as numbers grew, Brigid and faith-sharing teams went out to churches far and wide. Easter was an opportunity to minister to the extra numbers who came, and in one church a blind person, a consumptive, a leper and a deranged person were healed through Brigid's ministry. Once a leading figure asked Brigid to consecrate his new house. She had a 'word of knowledge' that he had never been baptised, so they had to postpone it until they could get a bishop to baptise him. After this, Patrick, recognising her strategic evangelistic role, arranged for an ordained person always to travel with her.

Once Brigid visited a place where the Christians feared to preach God's Word because of a madman. Brigid challenged the madman to preach the Word of God himself, which he did! She told nuns who saw the Devil: 'Make Christ's Cross on your face and on your eyes.'

Her unknown biographer writes: 'Her heart and mind were a throne of rest for the Holy Spirit. She was simple towards God; compassionate towards the wretched; she was splendid in miracles and marvels. . . .'

Someone in the ninth century composed a famous poem entitled 'Hail Brigid'. Its theme is the disappearance of the pagan world of Ireland and the triumph of Christianity. This was symbolised by the abandonment of the ancient hill-fort of Allen as the seat of the once powerful kings of Leinster, and its replacement by Brigid and her Kildare monastic network which had become the main source of blessing and protection for the people.

In later times Brigid was imagined to be the mid-wife, or the wet-nurse, present at Christ's birth, and she was made a symbol of the Bride of Christ. She became the guardian of the poor who work the land, and the patron of those who study. Beautiful prayers have come down to us which reflect these traditions.

Places to visit

Ireland: From Dublin: To Kildare. East of Kildare to the Curragh common land, still unfenced, in honour of Brigid whose monks cleared and farmed it.

England: Glastonbury which legend says she visited.

St David
1st March

Leader   ✠ In the name of the Creator of lights;
In the name of the Christ of the Cross;
In the name of the Spirit of the well-springs.

 There may be singing.

Leader   Great God, who called your servant David to be an
apostle and father in God to the people of Wales:
grant that, inspired by the fire of his faith, we too
may see divine fruit in our land, and receive the
crown of everlasting life.

All   Amen.

May All Things Praise You

from Llyfr Du Caerfyrddin (adapted).

Leader   Hail, glorious Lord!
May church and chancel praise you.

All   May valley floor and mountainside praise you.
May the well-springs praise you.
May night and day praise you.
May silk and fruit-tree praise you.

Leader   Abraham, founder of the Faith, praised you.

All   May eternal life praise you.
May birds and bees praise you.
May grass and fresh shoots praise you.

Leader   Aaron and Moses praised you.

All   May male and female praise you.
May the seven days and the stars praise you.

May the air and the upper atmosphere praise you.
May books and letters praise you.
May fishes in the river praise you.
May thought and action praise you.
May sand and soil praise you.

Leader May all the good that has been done praise you.
All We praise you, Lord of glory!
Hail, glorious Lord!

 The Word of God

Any of the following Bible passages may be read, interspersed with singing.

Reader *Psalm 26; Proverbs 4:10–27; 1 Thessalonians 2:2b–12.*

 A song

The Life of David

A reading from the Life of David (below) or from Rhigyfarch's Life.

Silence, teaching, sharing, or singing.

Prayers

Prayer of Sorrow:

Leader Lord, David worked with unflagging zeal:
All Forgive us for our flickering flame.

Leader Lord, David witnessed with unfaltering faith:
All Forgive us for our faltering steps.

Leader Lord, David served with unstinting generosity:
All Forgive us for our fickle friendship.

Prayer of Washing:

Leader   Lord, as fish live in water, so we live in your love.
All   Bathe us in your cleansing rivers.
   Soak us in your healing waters.
   Drench us in your powerful down-falls.
   Cool us in your bracing baths.
   Refresh us in your sparkling streams.
   Master us in your mighty seas.
   Calm us by your quiet pools.

Prayer of Intercession:

Leader   Teach us, our God and King, to love you in each
   and every person, to love by noticing the little
   things, to love by cherishing the little things, to
   love by serving in little things, to pray by offering
   the little things. . . .

Prayer of Dedication:

All   Lord our God, we would be true in all the work
   we do;
   All that is done, we do it unto you.
   We would be true in watch of day or night;
   Be vigilant and watch with only you in sight.
   We would be true in all the words we pray;
   Be heartfelt, caring, in all the words we say.
   We would be true in all from which we abstain;
   From boasting and greed we always will refrain.

There may be free prayer.

A hymn may be sung.

All   The grace of our Lord Jesus Christ, the love of God,
   and the fellowship of the Holy Spirit, be with us all
   evermore. Amen.

THE LIFE OF DAVID

David was born about AD 500 on the westerly tip of Pembrokeshire. He became a monk at Ty Gwyn under Abbot Paulinus, who had once assisted the famous Bishop Germanus in Gaul, and whom a tombstone described as 'a most holy fosterer of righteousness'.

The two of them sought God on an island. Paulinus told David God had called him to gather 'bundles of souls'. David gathered a mission team and established monastic centres in key places, as far as the English Midlands. This Mission Team gave four rules to the people: pray; watch; work; abstain from strong drink. David's followers became known as the 'Watermen' because, so people said, 'as fish live in water so these people live in God'.

David and three friends waited on God for further guidance in the shadow of the Black Mountains, where they built a chapel and cell where Llanthony Abbey now stands. They were guided by God to build a large, permanent centre in the valley where David was born, on the site near the modern St David's Cathedral.

Rhigyfarch, David's ninth-century biographer, described life at the monastery: 'They place the yoke upon their shoulders; they dig the ground tirelessly with mattocks and spades; they carry hoes and saws for cutting, and provide with their own efforts for all the needs of the community.'

They had all things in common, no one should even say 'This is my book.' Their clothing was basic, mainly skins. David upheld St Paul's rule: 'If a person will not work, he will not eat.' Although the brothers had only one proper meal each day, they prepared appetising meals for the sick and aged guests. The tenth-century Laws of Howell make clear that the monasteries were more a fellowship than a hierarchy. Though the abbot had particular responsibilities, gifts of money had to be shared equally between them all. The large monasteries were divided into households each of which had one priest.

David brought the best out of others, as when he encouraged

the timid Cynnyd to share fully in the conversation. He was generous towards those whose work seemed more successful: he offered accommodation to Justinian for his many new recruits. When the monastery's hive of bees threatened to emigrate to Ireland with brother Modomnic, David finally blessed their going: 'May the land to which you go abound with your offspring!'

David's daily recipe of prayer that wept before God, Holy Communion, and a bathe in cold water forged a passion and purity that was poured into teaching, counselling and practical work. He inspired team-work, even with critics. Gildas, the outspoken English church leader, criticised some of the practices of the 'Watermen', yet David invited him to stay and work things out in fellowship.

David's final words to the Christian people of Wales were: 'Be happy and keep your faith, and do the little things that you have heard and seen me do.' Another account adds: 'Always be of one mind. . . .' It was said that at his death 'kings mourned him as a judge, the older people as a brother, the younger as a father'.

After his death Wales continued to honour his memory. The monasteries influenced the pattern of life for centuries. Gerald in his *Description of Wales* states that the Welsh churches 'enjoy far greater tranquillity than elsewhere. For not only is protection assured for animals to pasture in churchyards, but also in boundaries far beyond.'

The nineteenth-century poet Gwenallt portrayed David as 'strolling from county to county like God's gypsy, with the Gospel and the Altar in his caravan . . . he brought the Church to our homes, and took bread from the pantry and bad wine from the cellar, and stood behind the table like a tramp so as not to hide the wonder of the Sacrifice from us. . . .'

Places to visit

St David's Cathedral and St Non's; Llanthony Abbey; Llandewi Brefi near Tregaron (where David refuted heresy); Henfynwyr near Cardigan Bay (where he was schooled).

St Chad

2nd March

Leader ✠ In the name of the God of thunder.
In the name of the Saviour from ill.
In the name of the Spirit of mercy.
In the name of the Three we are still.

Leader Father, your church gave you much glory through the holy life and pastor's zeal of your humble servant Chad. As we celebrate his heavenly birthday, may we profit from his example, and deepen our prayer, until we join him in the eternal homeland, through Jesus Christ our Lord.

 There may be singing.

 Psalm

Reader *Psalm 18:1–19.*

Chad of the Journey

Leader God of the storm, God of the stillness:
    All Of squalls of power and of shimmering calm.

Leader Into life's troughs and into life's billows:
    All Come with the reach of your long right arm.

Leader Chad of the journey, Chad of the prayer:
    All Of the humble heart and the teaching tales.

Leader Into life's troughs and into life's billows:
    All He brings God's Presence that prevails.

Leader	People of faith, Body of Christ:
All	Joined to the saints, joined to our Source.
Leader	In time of temptation, when tossed about:
All	We take heart from Chad's God, we finish our course.

The Word of God

Reader	*Isaiah 4:2–6.*

Leader	Mighty God, you are stronger than the elements:
All	Mighty God, you are stronger than the storm.
Leader	Mighty God, you are stronger than the tyrants:
All	Mighty God, you are stronger than the grave.
Leader	Each day, each dark, In time, in eternity, We are in your keeping sure:
All	We are in your keeping sure.

Reader	*Luke 14:7–11.*

The Life of Chad

(below)

Teaching, silence, preparation of role plays of prayer themes, or singing.

Prayers

Leader	Father, Chad showed us that a true leader is a servant; give us and our leaders a serving spirit, especially those in authority in industry and Government . . .

Father, Chad showed us that the headquarters of a church should be a place of prayer; we pray for the leadership of our churches. . . . We pray for the cathedral and diocese of Lichfield and for the

renewal of all churches throughout the English
Midlands. . . .

Father, Chad showed us how even the most
painful death can end in glory; we pray for those
who are nearing the end of their earthly journey:

Saviour and Friend, how wonderful art Thou;
My Companion upon the changeful way,
The Comforter of its weariness,
My Guide to the Eternal Town,
The welcome at its gate.

There may be silence or singing.

Leader   The Lord Christ go with you, wherever He may
send you,
May He guide through the wilderness, protect you
through the storm.
May He bring you home rejoicing at the wonders
He has shown you,
May He bring you home rejoicing once again into
our doors.

THE LIFE OF CHAD

Although Chad was a Saxon, he trained with his three brothers
at Aidan's monastery at Lindisfarne, and spent a period in
Ireland.

Chad was asked to become abbot of Lastingham after his
brother Cedd, who had founded it, died. Here he passed on
some of his own great store of learning, and was described as
an 'admirable teacher'.

Then he was made a bishop of the Northumbrians. Like Aidan
before him, he refused special honours and travelled by foot
rather than by horse. Humility was his hallmark. Archbishop
Theodore decided that Chad had not been consecrated a

bishop in the proper (i.e. Roman) manner. Chad's reply was that he had never considered himself worthy to be consecrated a bishop in the first place, and he readily offered to resign, in favour of the prestigious prelate Wilfred.

Theodore, however, was impressed by Chad's holy life and 'completed' his consecration. When a vacancy arose in the huge Diocese of Mercia (the English Midlands) Theodore appointed Chad, and personally lifted him on to a horse, so reluctant was Chad not to walk. Even at Lichfield, where Chad made his headquarters, he retained the simple way of prayer. He built some cells nearby which he and eight brothers would regularly retreat to. During this period Chad was known for his prophetic preaching, and he established a monastery at Barton, Lincolnshire.

Chad was respected for his disciplined lifestyle, his voluntary poverty, his teaching, his prayer, and his vivid sense of awe. Whenever he heard strong wind or thunder he would go and pray in the church until calm returned. When he was asked why he did this he quoted Psalm 18: 'The Lord thundered from the heavens and the voice of the Most High was heard.' 'Don't you realise,' Chad explained, 'that God sends wind, lightning and thunder to excite earth's peoples to fear him, to humble their pride and make them aware that they will be judged?'

Sadly, plague decimated his flock, or, in the words of Bede 'translated the stones of the church from their earthly places to the heavenly building'.Chad himself was given a week's notice that the plague was about to take him, too, for he heard inexpressibly sweet music of angels come from heaven into his oratory for half an hour and then ascend again to heaven. He informed his brothers that 'this amiable guest' was to take him, and he said his farewells. At his death his brother Cedd was seen coming with angels from heaven to greet him.

Places to visit

Lichfield Cathedral and cell; Lindisfarne; Lastingham.

St Patrick
17th March

A voice   Go and make disciples of all peoples, baptising them in the name of the Father, the Son, and the Holy Spirit. *(Matthew 28:19)*

Leader   The sun rises daily because you, O Lord, command it:

All   Its splendour will not last, created gods all perish.

Leader   Christ the true Sun nothing can destroy:

All   The Splendour of God, he shall reign for ever.

There may be a hymn or orchestral music.

Leader   Almighty Trinity, who in your providence chose your servant, Patrick, to be the apostle of the Irish, to boldly confront the kingdom of darkness, to baptise those who were lost and in error, and to bring them into the light and truth of your Word: give us his boldness, keep us in that light, and bring us to everlasting life, through Jesus Christ our Lord.

All   Amen.

Patrick's Breastplate

Leader   I arise today through a mighty strength, the strong name of the Trinity.

All   I arise today through the strength of Christ in His incarnation.

Leader	The strength of Christ in His baptism and His death on the Cross for my salvation;
All	His bursting from the burial tomb, His riding up the heavenly way;
Leader	Through the strength of His descent to the dead and His coming at the day of doom;
All	I arise today through God's strength to pilot me.
Leader	His might to uphold me, His wisdom to guide me, His ear to listen to my need.
All	God's shield to protect me, His host to secure me, alone or in a crowd.

The Word of God

Any of these Bible passages may be used.

Reader	*Psalm 5.*

Response after each stanza:

All	Lord, you surround the righteous with the shield of your favour.
Reader	*Hosea 2:19–23.*
Reader	*2 Corinthians 2:14–3:3.*
Reader	*Mark 10:28–31.*

Patrick's song 'Christ be beside me' may be sung (as adapted by J. Quinn SJ to the Gaelic tune Bunessan).

A reading from the Life of Patrick (below), silence, sharing or teaching.

All stand   **The Creed of St Patrick**

This may be read by one person or said by all.

Reader or *All*	There is no other God, or ever was, nor will be than God the Father unbegotten, without

beginning, from whom all things began, the Lord of the universe, as we have been taught; and His Son Jesus Christ, whom we declare always to have been with the Father, spiritually and ineffably begotten by the Father before the beginning of the world, before all beginning; and by Him were made all things seen and unseen. He was made human, and, having defeated death, was received into heaven by the Father; who has given Him all power over all names in heaven and on earth, and every tongue shall confess to Him that Jesus Christ is Lord and God, in whom we believe and whose coming we expect soon, to be judge of the living and of the dead; who will give back to every one according to their deeds. And He poured forth upon us abundantly the Holy Spirit, the gift and pledge of immortality, who makes those who believe and obey children of God and co-heirs with Christ, and Him do we confess and adore, one God in Trinity of the Holy Name.

There may be singing, teaching, creative writing, movement, prophesying or spontaneous praying that express the spirit of The Creed of St Patrick.

Patrick Prayers

There may be intercession groups for Ireland, introduced by this confession that Patrick taught all his followers to use repeatedly. Say or sing several times:

All   Kyrie eleison, Christe eleison
or
Lord have mercy, Christ have mercy.

Creative Activity

At longer St Patrick gatherings each of the following petitions may be allocated to a group to meditate on, discuss, dramatise or pictorialise. Alternatively, each petition may be used as a heading, and anyone is invited to pray on that theme.

Leader   Lord, give us grace to turn adversity into advance for you . . .
Lord, give us willingness to go anywhere for you . . .
Lord, give us winsomeness to woo a rising generation for you . . .
Lord, give us boldness to confront the seats of evil for you . . .
Lord, give us faithfulness, to surmount disappointments for you . . .
Lord, give us imagination to communicate the Truth for you . . .
Lord, give us holiness to conquer the corroding invasion of worldly charms.

We bring before you, Lord, the people of Ireland; may Irish people have one heart, one voice, one love for you, one mission to the world.
May British people make themselves one with their Irish brothers and sisters, in penitence and humble love.

We bring before you, Lord, the sighing of the prisoners, the sorrows of the bereaved, the needs of those who are hostile, the failing powers of the old.

Leader	The eternal Father,
	The eternal Spirit,
	The eternal Word,
	Shield you on every side,
	Protect you from every evil,
	And bring you to the land of promise.
All	Amen.

THE LIFE OF PATRICK

Patrick was born in western Britain, most probably in Cumbria, about AD 390. His father, Calpornius, was a Roman alderman who had a wealthy estate with male and female slaves. Although his grandfather was a Christian priest, it seems that Patrick and his parents were only nominal Christians. At the age of sixteen he was captured by pirates and sold as a slave in Ireland. He was denied the polished education he might otherwise have had, and instead tended his master's sheep on the hills of County Antrim. Those hills, however, turned him to Christ and gave him a priceless education in prayer and the Christian life. He tells us: 'More and more did the love of God, and my awe of him and faith increase. My spirit was moved so that in a single day I would say as many as a hundred prayers and in the night a like number, even when I was staying in the woods and in the mountain.'

Six years later God gave Patrick a 'word of knowledge': he had a mental picture of a boat ready to sail to Britain. He trekked 200 miles over unknown countryside before he found the boat and escaped. God put a longing in Patrick's heart to be one of his hunters, or fishers of souls. So he spent time in Auxerre, and was trained as a priest.

A decade or two after his return to Britain Patrick had a dream. . . . A messenger came with many letters and handed him one of them. Instead of the usual name of the writer on the opening page, Patrick read 'the voice of the Irish'. The Irish pleaded: 'Come and walk among us once more.' On another night an insistent voice within Patrick begged him to come to Ireland. When Patrick wondered whose was the voice, it replied: 'He who gave His life for you, He it is who speaks within you.' Patrick awoke full of joy, and made up his mind to go. Bishop Germanus, supported by the British Bishops, arranged for him to be sent as a missionary bishop to Ireland.

Ireland, which lay outside the protection of the Roman Empire, consisted of almost impenetrable bogs and forests. The population was about a quarter of a million. Constant warfare was normal. Few survived beyond the age of forty. Although a Bishop Palladius had been sent from Rome and had brought Christianity to an area in the south, this mission had not 'taken off'.

When Patrick arrived back in Ireland he established a church above Strangford Lough, and the Faith spread. In a stroke of inspired genius, he chose to celebrate his first Easter on the Hill of Slane. This was in full view of the place where the High King of Tara, with all his druids, lit a large fire to proclaim the rebirth of the sun after winter's death. Every other fire had to be extinguished until it was re-lit from this fire. So when Patrick lit a fire in the name of the risen Christ, the future of Ireland was at stake. 'If that fire is not quenched today it will burn for ever, and it will overcome all the fires of our religion', the druids told the High King. Many are the legends of how God used nature's wonders to extinguish the pagan fire and to protect Patrick's life.

His mission was unique and dangerous. He tells us the onslaughts on his person were 'too numerous for words'. Over 100 kings ruled over their independent kingdoms; Patrick worked to secure both their goodwill and their bodyguards for his preaching tours. Sometimes he first won the allegiance of younger members of a royal family, or of their mother; sometimes he paid the king money.

He also worked to win over or to outflank the poets, the lawyers and the druids, who advised the kings and were organised on a national basis. If he had a rapport with the poets, the majority of the druids seem to have opposed Patrick and the new religion. The Deer's Cry, or St Patrick's Breastplate, is an excellent example of the approach of Patrick as he tried to replace traditional charms with Christian faith.

Patrick probably established his headquarters at Armagh. He wrote two 'open letters' which survive. His 'Confession' was a defence against his critics; his 'Letter to Coroticus' was an appeal to the British chief who murdered Patrick's converts. Through these letters Patrick 'makes himself transparent to us to a very unusual extent. This can be said of no other British person in the whole of ancient history' (R. P. C. Hanson). In these writings Patrick is too modest to mention his great achievements. He comes across as a tireless missionary constantly on the move, whose mission bears lasting fruit. He wrote that a 'people of the Lord' was created, and 'the sons and daughters of the kings of the Irish are seen to be monks and virgins of Christ'. Patrick himself baptised thousands. Many others, he writes, were 'reborn in God through me and afterwards confirmed. Clergy were ordained for them everywhere, for a people just coming to the faith.'

Later biographers overlaid the real Patrick with legends from popular mythology. The real Patrick was a strong man of action with a deep spiritual nature, and an enthusiasm which enabled him to surmount all kinds of trials. A man of hard work and intensive prayer, he sacrificed his birthright, home, and everything he was humanly fond of in order to become 'the last of the apostles'. He glories in Christ at the fruit of his labours, which he sees not as his doing, but as the gift of God, of the Spirit that dwelt within him.

Places to visit

Ireland: Strangford Lough, The Hill of Slane, Croagh Patrick Mountain, Cashel, Armagh.

England: Glastonbury, which he or his namesake stayed at.

ST CUThBERT
20th March

Leader   ✠ In the name of the holy Father.
In the name of the victor Son.
In the name of the praying Spirit.
In the name of the Three-in-One.

Leader   King of heaven, who called Cuthbert from tending
sheep to be a shepherd of the people; help us,
inspired by his example, to win the godless, to
heal the sick, to guard unity, and to storm
heaven's gates, through Jesus Christ our Lord.

Leader   Holy God, holy and immortal:
     All   Your presence goes before us now.

Leader   God of the hills, God of the outposts:
     All   Your presence goes before us now.

Leader   God of the streets, God of the people:
     All   Your presence goes before us now.

 There may be singing.

Psalm 121

Reader   I lift up my eyes to the hills – where does my help
come from?
My help comes from the Lord, the Maker of
heaven and earth.
     All   He will not let you stumble – he who watches over
you will not sleep.

Reader	The protector of Israel never slumbers or sleeps.
All	The Lord will guard you; he is by your side to protect you. The sun will not hurt you by day, nor the moon by night. The Lord will protect you from all danger; he will keep you safe. He will protect you as you come and go, now and for ever.

The Word of God

Any of these passages may be read:

Reader   *1 Samuel 3:1–10.*

My Heart's Desire

Reader	My heart's desire is to serve the King, To heed his call in everything.
All	My heart's desire is to touch his cloak, To release his power in ordinary folk.
Reader	My heart's desire is to pray like flint, Till demons flee and winds relent.
All	My heart's desire is that sick are cured, And that hostile mockers praise the Lord.
Reader	My heart's desire is that Christians are one, In a church in peace and communion.
All	My heart's desire is to reach the throne, Where God reigns in glory with his own.

Reader   *2 Timothy 2:1–10.*

Reader   *Luke 9:1–6.*

The Life of Cuthbert

From The Life of Cuthbert (below) or from Bede's Life of Cuthbert.

There may be silence, teaching, creative arts, sharing, singing.

Prayers

At longer gatherings each of these five themes may lead into group or informal prayer:

Reader   A small infant sensed God's call on Cuthbert: Let us pray for the children in our homes, churches and neighbourhoods. May they be introduced to the Holy Spirit, attracted by holy lives, and respond to divine callings . . .

Reader   From being a winning athlete Cuthbert became an athlete of the spirit: Let us pray for Christians in sport, for all sports people, that they may see their training as a step towards the eternal race . . .

Reader   Cuthbert never flagged in his faith-sharing, love-sharing journeys to the unreached: Let us pray for those for whom the church seems inaccessible, that church people may reach out to them with infectious enthusiasm . . .

Reader   Cuthbert warned against schism and jealously guarded unity: Let us plead forgiveness for the schisms in the church today and pray that communion may be restored . . .

Reader   Our soldier of Christ ventured into the battlefields of the evil powers: Let us intercede that the powers of the elements, human and unseen powers that oppose God, may lose their hold and that Christ may be enthroned . . .

There may be singing.

Leader   Go forth in the spirit of Cuthbert;
          To storm heaven with your prayers;
          To welcome those in the household of faith;
          To eagerly walk God's saving ways;
          To live in love and peace with all.

All   The grace of our Lord Jesus Christ, the love of God,
         and the fellowship of the Holy Spirit be with us all,
         evermore. Amen.

THE LIFE OF CUTHBERT

As a boy Cuthbert was strong, acrobatic and spiritual. He was schooled by Kenswith, one of the first nuns in Northumbria, where he played and prayed well. He was a natural leader throughout his life.

Once he was with some shepherds on the Lammermuir hills, when he saw a vision of a holy person being taken to heaven in a trail of light. Next day he learned that Aidan, the much-loved leader of the Christian Mission based at Lindisfarne, had died. This had a great effect upon him. He went to the monastery at Melrose and offered himself for life-service. The prophetic abbot, Boisil, knew at first sight that God had sent someone special to the monastery.

Here Cuthbert not only excelled in work, prayer and study, just as he had excelled at athletics, he also excelled in his evangelistic endeavours. He visited every village and hamlet, however inaccessible, by foot, horse or boat, to explain the Christian Faith, to bring the people to deep and heartfelt conversion, and to bring healing to the people. He prepared for this ministry by night-long vigils of prayer and praise, sometimes immersed in the sea throughout!

He was invited to become the steward of Ripon monastery, where he showed the same zeal, not only for going out on missions, but also for hospitality. When travellers arrived cold, tired, and hungry, he would wash and warm their feet, and order their food himself.

He returned to Melrose. When the abbot died of the plague Cuthbert took his place. He, too, succumbed to the plague, but on learning that his monks had prayed for him all night he rose from his sick-bed. He recovered, though he limped for the rest of his life, and he ministered to survivors in the plague-ridden villages.

The Synod of Whitby in 664 decreed that the Roman rules and rites be imposed on all the Celtic churches. Some of Cuthbert's dearest brothers left Lindisfarne and returned broken-hearted to Ireland. Cuthbert was made prior and abbot of Lindisfarne. Just as he had earlier fought to preserve the local customs, so now Cuthbert fought to preserve unity in the church. He continued to model the Christ-like spirituality of the Celts in his relationships, prayer and outreach, but he insisted that all his monks adopt the calendar and customs decided upon at Whitby. The monks argued against these things, especially at having to change their varied dress for the dull uniformity of the Roman habit. When there was quarrelling at meetings, Cuthbert would walk out and resume next day, smiling as if nothing had happened. He kept a light touch.

Cuthbert did not let dissension deflect him from mission. He continued his prayer vigils, and his travels to bring the Gospel, the sacraments, and healing to the people. These were effective because he felt deeply; he wept over people's sins.

Yet these labours could not satisfy the deepest longing in his heart: to storm the gates of heaven until the unseen godless powers were dethroned. When he was not quite forty, he went to the rocky Inner Farne Island, to engage alone in uninterrupted spiritual battle. Of course, his brother monks, and others came for times of worship, counsel and healing, he grew a few things to eat, and the birds became his friends, but his prime work was intercession. This, to men and women of God like Cuthbert, was the front-line work in God's kingdom.

Not everyone agreed. A church synod presided over by Archbishop Theodore elected Cuthbert as Bishop of Hexham, and a delegation led by the King pressed him to accept. He knew this was God's will, for it fulfilled a prophecy given him years before, but he begged one more winter on his prayer island, and persuaded the authorities to change plans, so he could become monk-bishop of his beloved Lindisfarne instead. Though he was much venerated, and failing in strength, his work as bishop was one long mission just like the earlier ones: preaching, healing, absolving, soul-friending leaders, ministering to the poor and weak. Bede records many miracles told to him by eye-witnesses. After only two years Cuthbert knew that death approached, and returned to Farne Island where he died after a painful illness. His final message to his monks was to live in peace with one another, in unity with the one church, and to practise hospitality.

He died on 20th March 687. After his death, his cherished body was taken to various safe places, such as Cuthbert's Cave, near Chatton, to protect it from marauders. Years later the coffin was opened and it was found his body had not decomposed; this was seen as a miraculous sign. Miracles occurred at Cuthbert's tomb and his fame multiplied. His final burial place became a great shrine, and the city and cathedral of Durham, where millions still kneel at his tomb, stand today as tribute to his greatness.

Places to visit

Cuthbert's Isle at Lindisfarne, Melrose, Inner Farne Island, Cuthbert's Cave near Chatton, his tomb at Durham Cathedral. St Cuthbert's Way from Melrose to Lindisfarne.

St Brendan

16th May

Leader ✠ In the name of the sending Father.
In the name of the pilgrim Son.
In the name of the wind-like Spirit.
In the name of the Three-in-One.

Leader High king of land and sea:
All Wherever we go is yours.
Leader You led our forebears by cloud and fire:
All You lead us through the days and nights.
Leader You led St Brendan by sign and sail:
All Your presence goes before us now.

There may be singing.

Reader *Psalm 107:1–9; 23–32.*

Response after each verse:

All Give thanks to the Lord, who leads His people on.

Sorrow

Leader Brendan was willing to leave all and sail out into the unknown:
Forgive us for putting safety first.
Lord have mercy:
All Lord have mercy.

Leader Brendan sought to be of one mind with his brothers and sisters:
Forgive us for acting as if we know best.
Christ have mercy:
All Christ have mercy.

Leader   Brendan built communities of faith and love:
         Forgive us for fostering self-sufficient attitudes.
         Lord have mercy:
All   Lord have mercy.

Leader   Father we thank you for Brendan's adventures for
         Christ on sea and land; and his drawing together
         of families and friends into communities of love.
         Kindle in us a spirit of endless adventure and a
         love that forges fresh bonds of community.

 The Word of God

Reader   *Jonah 2.*

We Journey in your Love

Reader   Forgetting what is past, we look to the things
         unseen.
All   We journey in your light.

Reader   We leave behind our ties.
All   We journey with single hearts.

Reader   The sun shall not strike us by day, nor the moon
         by night.
All   We journey in your shielding.

Reader   We look not to right or left, but straight towards
         your way.
All   We journey in your truth.

Reader   The rough places shall be smoothed and the
         pitfalls shall be cleared.
All   We journey in your power.

Reader   The proud shall be brought low and the humble
         shall be raised up.
All   We journey in your justice.

Reader   The hungry shall be fed and the poor shall have
         good news.
All   We journey in your love.

| Reader | No final home have we on this life's passing seas. |
| All | We journey towards our eternal home. |

One or both of the following may be read:

Reader   *Acts 27:1–26 (or 14–26).*

Short silence or singing.

Reader   *John 21:1–14.*

The Life of Brendan

Reader   *A reading from The Life of St Brendan (below).*

Meditation, sharing, or activities.

Creative activities

Coracle making (miniature ones can be made out of half-nuts, matchsticks and card), sea journey paintings, or dramatic presentation of a Celtic boat song.

   There may be singing.

Prayers

Reader   I thank you for the ways you have led me.
I ask your help as I journey through difficult places.

All   Father be with us on every road,
Jesus be with us on every mound;
Spirit be with us through every stream,
Headland and ridge and round.

Reader   Protect those who work on the seas, those who travel by night, those who serve us in space, and our brothers or sisters who are making difficult journeys of faith.

All   Be in each sea, each town, each moor,
Each lying down, each rising up;
In the trough of the billows, in the wastelands of sin,
Each step of the journey we take.

There may be free prayer for people on journeys.

Leader   Jesus who stopped the wind and stilled the waves,
grant you calm in the storm times;
Jesus victor over death and destruction bring safety
on your voyage;
Jesus the purest love, perfect companion, bring
guarding ones around you;
Jesus of the miraculous catching of fish, and the
perfect lakeside meal, guide you finally ashore.

 There may be singing.

Leader   The God of life be your champion and leader.
You shall not be left in the hand of the wicked;
You shall not be bent in the court of the false;
You shall rise victorious above them
As rise victorious the crests of the waves.
All   We'll go forth with the vision of God;
We'll sail into God's ocean of love.

There may be sea music, movement or singing.

THE LIFE OF BRENDAN THE NAVIGATOR

Brendan was born at Annagh, Tralee Bay, in southern Ireland about 486 and lived to be over ninety. The Christianity Patrick had spread through Ireland had inspired almost every local community to focus its life on a friendly monastery; people were alive with the freshness of God. Before he was born Brendan's mother dreamed that her womb was full of pure gold. On the night of his birth Erc, the local bishop, saw the village 'all in one great blaze', with angels in shining white garments all around it. Realising this was a child marked out for a special destiny, he asked a nun called Ita to foster Brendan. When he was old enough Erc himself taught Brendan the Bible, and Brendan learned all about the saints who were the glory of Ireland. The order of events in his life is not clear, but it seems he was ordained a priest, became a monk, and gathered others around him in a new monastic community life.

Jesus' teaching that everyone who has left family or possessions for His sake would receive a hundredfold and inherit eternal life spoke deeply to Brendan; a love for the Lord grew in his heart so strong that he desired to leave all and seek some land of promise far from human clamour. This led to the famous voyages of Brendan the navigator, which inspired storytellers for centuries to come. Someone in the tenth century wrote down these stories.

Once, Brendan asked his friend Barinthus, grandson of the great King Niall, to encourage him with some words from God. Barinthus told how his son had walked out on him, but had stumbled upon an island of monks, and now God was working miracles through him. Barinthus visited his son there. The monks lived their individual lives in separate cells, but they would come out of their cells like a swarm of bees to welcome a stranger; there was no divisiveness in their talk, or in their friendship. While they were there, Barinthus and his son discovered an island of saints radiant with the light of Christ. This they briefly visited, but they were told not to stay.

Brendan was captivated. He took fourteen brothers into a retreat to wait on God, and his family fasted and prayed too. They all agreed God wanted Brendan to sail to this 'land of Promise'. Eventually sixty people left in three large coracles piled with necessities.

After skirting round or visiting various islands, some inhabited by holy hermits who prophesied over them, surmounting whirlpools and riding on dolphins, Brendan and his crew returned to Ireland. They gathered strength for a second voyage, which included hair-raising experiences, illness, death, fellowship with island hermits, and a charming rapport with creatures of sea and land.

After seven hard years they found an island on which lived a holy man, clothed, like Adam, in naked innocence, which they took to be the island of paradise. This holy man helped them understand that if they settled there, they would spoil the innocence of the island, and bring speech, and with it sin; he urged them to return. One senses Brendan returned a chastened, even angry man. It seems it took some years for him to come to terms with his 'shadow' side, and there are stories of his 'taking it out' on others. Ita wisely advised him to travel abroad. God began to work miracles through him, and he founded monasteries, in Britain and Gaul. During various visits home and away it is said he met with both St Brigid and St Columba who perhaps acted as spiritual guides.

Brendan mellowed. He became a major, though unsmiling, Christian leader. He founded the great Clonfert Monastery, which attracted three thousand brothers. He wrote an inspired Rule of Life which was used for several hundred years. He died while on a visit to his sister Brig. At Mass the Sunday before he died, he said: 'God is calling me to the eternal kingdom; and my body must be taken to Clonfert, for angels will attend there, and there will be my resurrection.' A prophet spoke of 'Brendan who was without crime, who was sage, and prophet and priest; ninety-three years exactly; he lived among great peril'.

Places to visit

Around Ireland's Dingle Peninsula: Mount Brandon where Brendan fasted forty days; Brandon Bay, whence he set sail. From Waterville – by boat to the Celtic monastic remains at Skellig Michael. Clonfert.

Sт Columba

9тh June

Leader ✠ Let the islands sing God's praise. *(Isaiah 42:12)*

🎼 *God's praises may be sung.*

Leader In the name of the sending Father.
In the name of the Son of the call.
In the name of the Dove descending.
In the name of the One in All.

Leader Kindle in us, O God, the flame of that love which
never ceases, that it may burn in us, giving light to
others. May that light which shone so brightly in
Columba, take away the darkness of our hearts,
and bring us to share with him the light of the
eternal city.

Leader Let us bless God in words that echo those of
Columba:

O God you are the Father of all who have believed:
From whom all hosts of angels have life and power
received.

All O God you are the Maker of all created things:
The righteous Judge of judges, almighty King of
kings.

Leader High in the heavenly city you reign as God adored:
And in the coming glory you shall be sovereign
Lord.

All You shine beyond our knowing, the everlasting
Light:
Unfaltering in loving, immeasurable in might.

Leader To humble and to poor ones your secrets you
unfold:
It's you who brings forth all things, all things both
new and old.

All I walk secure and fruitful in every coast or clime:
In name of Father, Saviour, and holy Dove
sublime.

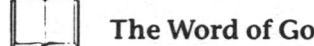 **The Word of God**

Reader *Psalm 34:1–18.*

*All respond after each stanza with these last words
that Columba transcribed:*

All Those who seek the Lord lack no good thing.

Reader *Lamentations 3:19–33.*

A Litany of Turning the Back

Leader Columba turned his back on his beloved Ireland
to show he repented for his part in violence to the
land, and to win as many converts to Christ's
kingdom in a new land as had perished in war. In
the spirit of Columba we pray:

I turn my back, Lord, on ill-will, envy, malice;
I leave behind regrets and bitter traits.
I turn my back, Lord, on possessiveness and
grasping;
I leave behind my headstrong foolish ways.
I turn my back, Lord, on misuse of earth and
people;
I leave behind my heedless, selfish days.

Leader The God of peace give us his pardon,
and fill us with the sweetness of his grace.

Reader *1 Corinthians 14:1–8.*

All   Lord, you are my island, in your bosom I nest.
You are the calm of the sea, in that peace I rest.
You are the deep ocean waves, with their sound
I sing.
You are the sound of the birds, in that tune
I hymn.
You are the white strand of the shore, on you
I gaze.
You are the swell breaking on the rocks, with them
I give praise.

*The Gospel of Luke 9:51–56 may be read at a
Communion Service.*

 There may be singing.

The Life of Columba

Reader   *An extract from the Life of Columba (below).*

*Teaching, creative arts, silence, discussion, dialogue or
singing.*

 Prayers

Leader   Circle me, Lord –
Keep fear without, keep joy within.
Keep complaining out, keep peace within.
Keep despair without, keep hope within.
Keep deceit without, keep beauty within.

All   Circle me, Lord. Amen.

Leader   Columba's voice echoed across the Isles:
Reader   Lord, may the voice of your servants sound clear
above the clamour of our times.

Leader   Columba converted new peoples and leaders:
Reader   We pray for the conversion of new cultures and
opinion-formers today.

Leader	He established many Christian communities and places of learning:
Reader	Lord, may truth and excellence flourish in such places today.

Leader	He extolled hard physical labour:
Reader	Bless all who do manual work today.

Leader	Columba joyed in creation:
Reader	Lord, give us, too, that joy.

Leader	Columba was angry at injustice:
Reader	May we stand for honesty in government, business and law.

Leader	Prophecy, purity and poetry flourished in Columba's life:
Reader	May these three virtues blossom throughout the church today.

Leader	Columba's departing to the heavenly country was glorious:
Reader	Grant us, too, Lord a quiet and glorious end.

| Leader | We pray to you for Iona. . . . We pray for Scotland to find her well-being in Christ, to rejoice in her Christian roots, to release her enemies from judgment, and to become a nation led by God, a shining mission-place among the nations. |

 There may be singing.

Leader   *(to be said at morning worship):*
Dearest Lord –
Be a bright flame before us;
Be a guiding star above us;
Be a smooth path beneath us;
Be a kindly shepherd behind us;
Today and always.

Leader   *(to be said at evening worship):*
The peace of Columba be yours in the smooth and
in the rough;
The big heart of Columba be yours in your going
and returning;
The God of Columba shield you and yours now
and always.

THE LIFE OF COLUMBA

Columba was a towering, contradictory figure born at Garton, in the north, into one of the great families of sixth-century Ireland. He was a brilliant organiser, yet a poet and song-writer; an impetuous and resourceful warrior who became a Christian statesman; a fierce prophet who developed the tender simplicity of his Master; a master strategist for the Kingdom of God.

Baptised as Crimthan (the wolf) and used to being served as a privileged lord, when he was quite young he entered a monastery and was given the name Colum (the dove). He moved from Moville monastery to Clonard, the most famous monastery in Ireland, founded by Finnian, where he was ordained a priest. He returned north and spent some fifteen years establishing up to 300 churches and monasteries throughout his home region. Derry, which fed a thousand visitors a day, and Durrow were famed for their influence and reflected Columba's love of learning.

Once, during a visit to Finnian, Columba secretly copied a beautifully inscribed book of Psalms without permission. Finnian challenged his presumption in the court of the king of Tara. King Diarmait delivered a verdict that is famous in copyright law: 'To every cow belongs her calf.' Clan wars were second nature in an Ireland only recently Christianised, and a ghastly slaughter took place on both sides in a battle against Diarmait's followers. A deeply penitent Columba decided to make restitution by bringing Christ's new life to as many pagans in another land as had lost their life in his own land. He had chosen the way of 'white martyrdom' – exiling himself from his home land. So he sailed to Iona, which his relative Conall, a ruler in Argyll, offered him.

The Isle of Iona became the largest Christian centre in the north of Britain, with thousands of male monks. Much of the highlands of Scotland were evangelised from there. Brude, a Pictish chief, whose dead child Columba raised to life, was converted. As a result the Faith spread wider still. Daughter monastic houses were founded. The hard manual labour and excellence in scripting at Iona brought work to the area.

Columba wrote many poems and songs, and his strong voice could be heard afar as he sang on his evangelising voyages. His prayers and blessings were powerful, and brought cures to sick people, animals and crops. His prophecies, which were all in the context of spiritual warfare, were accurate in extraordinary detail: he foretold the exact time two boys would die, the appearance of a whale, the arrival and names of visitors to Iona, future occupants of thrones, the downfall of evil people. He was familiar with the world of the supernatural, and encountered angels. He also had political acumen and a strong sense of strategy. His influence on the life of Scotland through his connection with the royal houses was great.

In 597 Columba knew his death was near, climbed the hill overlooking the monastery, blessed the brothers, and prophesied over Iona. He called it a 'thin place' (meaning heaven and earth are only thinly separated there), and predicted it would return to a mere grazing place, but that one day it would be restored. This is being fulfilled in our time.

After his death Adamnan, a successor as abbot of Iona, wrote an account of his miracles and prophecies, and Iona monks spread the Faith to new places in Scotland, Ireland, Iceland, and Italy. From Iona, Aidan and other monks journeyed south to Lindisfarne, and established a base, inspired by the life and disciplines of Columba, that was to have immeasurable influence in England.

Places to visit

Scotland: Iona.

Ireland: Glencolumcill (his birthplace in Donegal), Kells Cathedral (the site of his monastery where the Book of Kells was inscribed), Clonard, Derry.

St Samson

28th July

---

*At longer gatherings the Life of Samson (below) may
be read before worship begins.*

Leader Light and peace has come into the world through
our Lord Jesus Christ and through His saints.

This response by all may be said or sung:

All The light of Christ has come into the world.

Leader You led your people of Israel to freedom by a pillar
of cloud by day and a pillar of fire by night.

All The light of Christ has come into the world.

Leader You led your people of this land out of darkness
through the holy prayers and powerful signs of
Samson and other saints.

All The light of Christ has come into the world.

Leader May we who walk in the light of your presence
acclaim your Christ, rising victorious, as He
banishes all darkness from our lives and from our
land today.

All The light of Christ has come into the world.

There may be singing.

The Word of God

Psalm

Reader *Psalm 125.*

Leader	We bless you Lord that Samson's birth, schooling and calling were the fruit of prophecy. We thank you that his prayer, his heroic acts of witness, his courtesy and wonderful love towards all, won pagans to the Faith, and patterned a new way of being the church. As we contemplate his life, give us a new zeal, we pray, through Jesus Christ. Amen.
Reader	*Judges 13:1–7; 24–25.*

The Song of Zechariah

Leader	Blessed are you, Lord, the God of Israel: You have come to your people and set them free.
All	You have raised up for us a mighty Saviour Born of the house of your servant, David.
Leader	Through your holy prophets, you promised of old To save us from our enemies, From the hands of all who hate us:
All	To show mercy to our forebears And to remember your holy covenant.
Leader	This was the oath God swore to our father, Abraham, To set us free from the hands of our enemies:
All	Free to worship you without fear, Holy and righteous before you All the days of our life.
Leader	And you, child, Shall be called the prophet of the Most High, For you will go before the Lord to prepare the way:
All	To give God's people knowledge of salvation By the forgiveness of their sins.
Leader	In the tender compassion of our God The dawn from on high shall break upon us:
All	To shine on those who dwell in darkness And the shadow of death, And to guide our feet into the way of peace.

Reader *Acts 28:1–10.*

Leader In faith I trust in the God of power:
All God is my refuge, a very strong tower.

*In a Communion service the Gospel of Luke 9:37–43
may be read.*

The Life of Samson

*The Life of Samson (below) or extracts from his
biography are read here if they were not read before
worship began.*

*There may be teaching, singing, and groups may
prepare to act out each of the following prayers.*

Prayers

Leader Thrice-holy God, eternal Three-in-One,
Make your people holy, make your people one.
Stir up in us the flame that burns out pride and
power.
Restore in us the love that brings the servant heart
to flower.
Thrice-holy God, come as the morning dew.
Hold up in us your love, which draws all lesser
loves to you.

Guard my eyes for me, Jesus Son of Mary,
lest seeing another's wealth makes me covetous.
Guard for me my ears lest they listen to slander.
Guard for me my tongue that it spread not gossip.
Guard for me my hands that they be not stretched
out for quarreling.
Guard for me my feet lest, bent on profitless
errands, they abandon rest.

Call, call, call, great Chief of the high hills.
Call, call, call, great Christ of the far paths.
Call, call, call, great Counsellor of the near gate.
Set our spirits free to soar where'ere you climb.
Set our feet free to trek where'ere you go.
Set our mouths free to say what'ere you command.

In the strength of the Warrior of God I oppose all that pollutes.
In the eye of the Face of God I expose all that deceives.

In the energy of the Servant God I bind up all that is broken.

There may be free prayer or singing.

A Blessing

Leader   The mantle of God be upon you
Wherever your feet shall tread.
The mantle of Christ to shade you from your crown to your sole.
The mantle of the Dove be upon you
To be your Blessing and Guide.

THE LIFE OF SAMSON

Almost every book in the Old Testament contains a warning: how easy it is for God's people to backslide. Almost every book also features a warrior of faith, raised up by God to restore Him as sovereign amongst His people. That pattern repeats itself in the history of the Christian church, not least in its beginnings here in Britain.

Dedicated Christians spread the Faith here when the Romans ruled most of what is now England. There were bishops in AD 314 who were doubtless holy men of God. But in 323 the Emperor Constantine espoused Christianity, and in 386 it became the official religion: from then on the slick and the slack people, not the saints, sought the status of clergy. By the time of Samson, it was unusual to find a clergyman who did not get drunk.

The holiness of the church was kept alive by people such as Bishop German, who came from Auxerre on missions. He encouraged British Christians to follow the example of people in the east of the Empire who left the decadent cities to live holy lives in remote places. So many did this in Britain that by the sixth century much of the church took the form of monastic communities; though even some of these were quite slack.

The most famous monastery in Britain was at Llantwit Major, near Cowbridge in Wales, founded by St Illtud, a great teacher and spiritual guide. It was here that the boy Samson was schooled.

Samson was probably born in 486. His father, Amon, and his mother, Anna were officials in neighbouring kings' courts, and they were Christians. Anna was infertile, but longed for a child. One day they travelled three days to see a prophet. Before they opened their mouths, he knew they wanted him to predict they would have a baby. He, however, wanted them to give their will to God first of all. He asked Amon to have made a rod of silver which was the exact height of his wife, and give it to God. After Amon had done that, he told them, God would give them a child. Then God told Anna in a dream that she would have a son; he would be a priest, and they were to name him Samson. No doubt this implied that he, like the Samson in the Old Testament, whose birth also came as a result of prophecy, would be strong for the Lord.

The Life of Samson is thought to have been written in the seventh century, not long after his death. Samson's nephew handed down much eye-witness material. It is therefore one of the earliest records of life in Britain.

The author mentions that Samson's parents took time to play creatively with him when he was an infant. That is something all children need, but so few receive. Since there were no state schools, Amon and Anna took him to Illtud's monastery school, where he learned the Psalms, philosophy, sports, and the ways of Christ. Illtud was regarded as the wisest man of his time. Yet we learn that when he and Samson debated the meaning of Scriptures, it was Samson who decided to fast and pray until understanding was given. He was the model of a serious Bible student.

And Samson proved to be ahead of the other monks in the school of faith. A monk was dying from a snake bite, and the brothers were grieving. Samson, however, asked permission to pray over him for healing. Illtud thought he meant to use magic charms as used by druid pagans, but Samson simply assumed that since Jesus healed sick people his followers should follow His command to do the same. The brother was cured, and that began a healing ministry in the church of Samson's time.

Samson grew in stature, and the time came when he was ordained deacon by Bishop Dubricius. Both Dubricius and Illtud saw the anointing of the Holy Spirit come upon him and stay upon him, in the form of a dove. These Celtic Christians were sensitive to these anointings, which often indicated to them who they should ordain.

Illtud's nephews had thought they would become the leaders of the monastery, because in those days leadership often went along the lines of heredity. The obvious stature of Samson threatened their ambitions. They were jealous, and they hatched a plot to poison him. God revealed to Samson what they were up to, and gave Samson supernatural protection. Later, the plotters confessed and were forgiven.

When his father almost died, Samson persuaded his entire family to take vows and enter monastic life. It was revealed to his mother that he would be the founder of many monasteries, which he was.

In due course Samson went to Ireland; then he was made a bishop. In those days bishops were not weighed down with bureaucracy, they were flying bishops. God's Spirit led Bishop Samson, after short stays at Caldey Island and Padstow, to journeys of witness in Cornwall, the Channel Islands, and then to found monasteries across the Channel in Brittany. His monastery at Dol became large and famous, and it was a monk there who wrote his life.

Places to visit

Wales: Llantwit Major, Caldey Island.

Brittany: Dol.

Channel Islands: St Samson's Church, Guernsey.

GLASTONBURY SAINTS
31st July

Leader   May the Holy Thorn of Glastonbury, sprung from
Arimathean Joseph's staff,
In winter's dark and summer's light proclaim the
birth of Christ – the true Sun.

The following may be said or sung:

Leader   The light of Christ has come into the world.
All   The light of Christ has come into the world.

Leader   Britain's Jerusalem, clothe yourself in the
garments of Christ.

Reader   *Psalm 122.*

All may repeat this phrase after every second verse:

All   Peace be within you, Jerusalem.

The Word of God

Any of these readings may be used.

Reader   *Isaiah 62:1–5.*

(At close): May these islands receive afresh the
beams of light, the heartfelt sharings, of Christ,
the true Sun.

Sorrow

Leader   We weep for the sins that have driven you from
your dwelling place:
For pride and prejudice;

For domination and division;
For belittling young or old, women or men – your
children all;
For abuse of your creation;
For worshipping what you created instead of you
alone;
For not welcoming the stranger and the needy.

*There may be silence or an activity that expresses
sorrow.*

Reader *John 19:38–42.*
(At close): May our islands receive afresh the
beams of light, the heartfelt sharings, of Christ,
the true Sun.

 There may be singing.

Reader *Acts 7:59–8:4.*

Leader After Jerusalem's Christians were scattered the
entomber of Christ, the noble commander Joseph,
the enlightener of Britain, so it is said, planted
here the Tree of Salvation.
Gildas the Wise, first writer of the Britons,
recounted for us, in Tiberius' last year, the coming
of the Light.
In these islands, stiff with pagan coldness, the
Sun's rays shone.

Reader With Aristobulos, first Bishop of Britain, fanning
the bright flame of Joseph's kindling,
Fagan and Dyfan, for King Lucius the Glorious,
restored here the church built by Christ's apostles'
hands.

Leader Set in the jewel of Avalon, a church of wattles was
        made by holy hands,
        Dedicated by command of Christ to the dearest
        Mother of God,
        That in these northern lands this first of churches
        should honour her who brought humanity's
        fullness to birth.

 There may be singing.

Prayer

Reader We give thanks for this cradle place of faith,
        Which drew to it, so 'tis said,
        Patrick and holy Irish hermits;
        Brigid and her winsome faith;
        David and his fiery zeal;
        Columba and his mighty prayers;
        Which draws to it still a multitude – saints,
        sinners, strangers – seekers all.

        May the Christ of the cosmos also be to this
        multitude the Christ of the womb, the workshop
        and the wounds; may this Christ of the
        resurrection live in our bodies now and for ever.
   All Amen.

Reader As we enter a new millennium we pray for the
        withering of gods that fail us. We pray that these
        seven jewels may shine from Britain's Jerusalem:
        Penitence • Praise;
        Holiness • Hospitality;
        Forgiveness • Justice;
        Healing.

        *This may be followed by teaching, discussion or
        singing.*

*At longer gatherings each of these jewels may be
expressed through creative activities such as pictures,
mime, clay, writing, music or prayer corners.*

Reader   Here may:
            The earth be cherished,
            The Faith be cradled,
            Energies be released for God.

Reader   Here may:
            Seekers be drawn to the eternally Real,
            And wanderers find their home in Christ.

Leader   From the thorn of Glastonbury may the goodness
            of creation blossom;
            From the thorn of past pride may loving
            friendships bloom;
            From the thorn of unquiet spirits may angelic
            harmonies burst forth.
            May Mary's Son live amongst us, and the Sacred
            Three encircle us always.

            ✛ In the name of the Lord of the elements.
            In the name of earth's Risen Son.
            In the name of the transforming Spirit.
            Eternally Three-in-One.

St Oswald

5th August

Onward Christian Soldiers

Leader   Young Oswald on Iona, learning ways of God:
Young Oswald on Iona, under yoke of work and
Word.

All   King Oswald in Northumbria, reflecting ways of
God:
King Oswald in Northumbria, winning subjects to
his Lord.

Leader   Onward Christian soldiers, from training grounds
of prayer:
With shield of faith march into new lands to
cleanse and clear.

All   Onward Christian soldiers, slay feuding, fear and
strife:
Bring to the land long blighted, Christ's truth and
love and life.

Leader   Onward Christian soldiers, prepare God's friends a
home:
With tongue of fire assist them as through the
land they roam.

All   Onward Christian soldiers, have mercy on the
poor:
And give to all who serve Christ an ever open
door.

Leader   Onward Christian soldiers, teach folk to live and
die:
Confident in heaven, re-born eternally.

Sorrow

Leader Oswald used every opportunity to bring Christ to others;
Forgive us for neglecting our opportunities.
Lord, have mercy:

All Lord, have mercy.

Leader Oswald used his wealth and position to serve the common good;
Forgive us for misuse of money and status.
Christ, have mercy:

All Christ, have mercy.

Leader Oswald showed valour and mercy in life and death;
Forgive us our selfish, cowardly ways.
Lord, have mercy:

All Lord, have mercy.

Reader *Psalm 72:1–7, 12–20.*

Response after verses 5, 7, 14, 17:

All May the King be like rain on the fields.

All Glory to the High King.
Glory to His Son.
Glory to His Spirit.
Ever Three-in-One.

There may be singing.

Prayer

Leader High King of heaven, who raised up Oswald to plant the healing tree of Christ's passion in his kingdom, redeem our land from the curse of disobedience and bring it into the wholeness of your just and gentle rule, through Jesus Christ our Lord.

Reader *Old Testament reading. Deuteronomy 17:14 –19.*

Reader   *New Testament reading. 1 Timothy 2:1–7.*

In a Communion Service the Gospel of Matthew 10:32, 40–42 may be read.

 There may be singing.

The Life of Oswald

Teaching or reading from the Life of Oswald, below.

 Creative Activity

Practise using hands in the prayers. Palms are turned upwards in praise as Oswald's often were. Hands are raised in royal blessing. Prayer of the valiant witness: Oswald died amid the slaughter of the battlefield praying 'God save these souls'. Re-enact this, lying down as if about to die, and write prayers for the souls of others.

 There may be singing.

 Prayers

Prayers of the Royal Hands in Praise
With these hands we praise you for the wonder of your world;
With these hands we praise you for protecting us from evil;
With these hands we praise you for our nurture in the Faith.

Prayers of the Royal Hands in Blessing
With these hands I bless the lonely, the forgotten and the lost;
With these hands I shield your messengers from attacks within, without;
With these hands I dispel darkness and rebuke the evil forces;
With these hands I pray your victory for those who fight for right.

Prayer of the Valiant Witness

My God, save the souls of those who destroy their
enemies;
My God, save the souls of those who destroy the
natural world;
My God, save the souls of those who destroy
reputations;
My God, save the souls of those who destroy the
unborn;
My God, save the souls of the victims one and all.

For healing of the land

Leader   We bring to you the lands of crop and dairy;
All   May these be seen as heaven's field.

Leader   We bring to you the lands of town and homestead;
All   May these be seen as heaven's field.

Leader   We bring to you the lands of work and commerce;
All   May these be seen as heaven's field.

Leader   We yield to you the lands of play and pleasure;
All   May these be seen as heaven's field.

For people in authority

High King of heaven and earth, from whom all
authority flows, may the diverse authorities of our
times acknowledge you as the Source of life,
emulate you as the Servant King, and fear you as
the Judge of truth.
We pray this especially for our local and national
Government, the European Parliament, the United
Nations – may these be inspired by Christian
values.

Blessing

Leader   May heaven's King go with you;
May Christ's Cross grow in you;
May the Spirit's fire glow in you
Till the final victory dawns.

THE LIFE OF OSWALD

When Oswald's father, the pagan King Aethelfrith of Northumbria, was killed in battle, his family had to flee or else they, too, would be killed. The island of Iona, in western Scotland, had gained a reputation as a sanctuary and place of learning under Columba, the royal founder of its monastery, and some unknown friend arranged for the royal children to be brought up there. At Iona they were taught the Christian faith and baptised; Oswald dedicated his whole life to Christ.

After seventeen years at Iona, Oswald learned that his uncle, Northumbria's King Edwin, had been killed and his kingdom was being desecrated by the pagan usurper King Cadwallon. Cadwallon killed Oswald's elder brother, who had first renounced his Christian faith. Oswald, however, collected a small army to confront Cadwallon at a place near Hexham, and the night before the battle (9th June) he erected a wooden cross in the ground, to show he fought, and intended to reign, as a Christian. There he knelt with his soldiers and prayed to God for victory, 'for he knows we have undertaken a just war for the safety of our nation'. Columba appeared to him in a dream and promised him victory. He won the battle, and the place, still marked by a cross, is known as Heavenfield to this day.

From his headquarters at Bamburgh, Oswald sent messengers to Iona inviting them to send a mission team. The first team failed, but the second, led by Aidan, began the conversion of Northumbria.

Oswald gave Aidan land at Lindisfarne where he established his Christian Centre, translated Aidan's words into the Northumbrian dialect, and made him a welcome guest at the castle.

Oswald was himself a man of prayer, who rose early every morning to make his devotions after matins. He was also a man of compassion, who on one occasion gave not only the royal food, but the silver plates, to the beggars at the gates. And he was a man of valour. In his final battle against the tyrant Penda, at a town (probably Oswestry) in Shropshire, his dying prayer was for his soldiers: 'May God have mercy on their souls'. He died on 5th August 642, aged thirty-eight.

Oswald's reign was short, but God-inspired, bold, energetic and civilising. Kingdoms of Britain speaking four different languages, British, Pictish, Irish and Anglo-Saxon were linked together for the first time under his influence. He provided breathing space for perhaps the most significant mission ever to the English people to get under way. His personal influence also continued after his death. It seems it had seeped into the very earth, which perhaps offers clues to the healing of our diseased land today. A sick horse and a sick girl were cured by touching the soil upon which Oswald met his death; the soil from that spot seemed to have power to make the grass grow greener, to resist fire and to heal all sorts of people who were touched by it. Others were healed when chips or moss from the Heavenfield cross were placed upon them, or by contact with Oswald's burial place. Bede comments: 'It is not surprising that the prayers of that king, who now reigns with the Lord, have great influence with Him, since during his reign as a king on earth he always gave precedence, in his work and his prayers, to the Kingdom which is eternal.'

Oswald's severed head was taken to Lindisfarne and was later placed in St Cuthbert's tomb at Durham Cathedral; other relics were preserved at Bamburgh.

In succeeding centuries peoples throughout Europe longed for examples of Christian kingship, and Oswald became a model far and wide. Many churches in the European Union are dedicated to St Oswald.

Places to visit

Bamburgh church and castle; Heavenfield and St Oswald's Church Wall, near Hexham; the parish churches of St Oswald at Durham and Oswestry; Iona.

St Ninian

26th August

Leader	The people who walked in darkness have seen a great light. Light has come into the world through Christ our High King; light has come into dark places through His saints.
All	The light of Christ has come into the world.
Leader	You led your people through Moses to a pillar of fire: you led your people through Ninian to a place of shining brightness.
All	The light of Christ has come into the world.
Leader	May we who walk in the light of your presence acclaim your Christ, that He may banish all darkness from our lives and our land today.
All	The light of Christ has come into the world.

There may be singing.

Leader	Thank you for the faith that led Ninian to witness to you in a land ignorant of your ways. Thank you for his vision of a Christian community to be a light in a dark place. Thank you for his courage to pray for miracles; and that a Shining House of the Lord was established on our soil. Give us such faith, vision and courage, and establish the work of our hands for the new millennium, through Jesus Christ our Lord.

The Word of God

Psalm

Reader   *Psalm 56.*

Response after verses 4, 7, 11, and 13:

All   I walk in the light that shines on the living.

All   Amen.

Reader   *2 Chronicles 5.*

Almighty God, Creator

Leader   Almighty God, Creator, greyness has enveloped
our world.

All   As we lift our hearts to you may your glory make
all things clear.

Leader   Almighty God, Creator, you seem absent from
your world.

All   Sun of suns, in everything we touch and everyone
we meet, light up your presence.

Reader   Almighty God, Creator, awake for us your
presence in cloud and grey and storm.

All   Till our trivial tasks become sacraments in the
temple of your love.

Reader   *2 Peter 1:10–19.*

*In a Communion Service the Gospel of Mark 9:2–13
may be read.*

This Catechism attributed to Ninian may be said:

Leader   What is best in this world?

All   To do the will of our Maker.

Leader   What is his will?

All   That we should live according to the laws of His
creation.

Reader	How do we know those laws?
All	By study – studying the Scriptures with devotion.

Reader	What tool has our Maker provided for this study?
All	The intellect which can probe everything.

Reader	And what is the fruit of study?
All	To perceive the eternal Word of God reflected in every plant and insect, every bird and animal, and every man and woman.

There may be singing.

The Life of Ninian

The Life of Ninian (below) may be read, and there may be teaching, discussion and singing.

Creative activity

Three groups could each act out one of the vices and its opposite virtue referred to in the prayer that follows.

Prayers

Reader	In Ninian there was nothing of fear, all was love; Forgive us for the places in our lives where fear has driven out love. Lord have mercy.
All	Lord have mercy.

There may be silence or free prayer on this theme.

Reader	In Ninian truth, holiness and warmth shone forth; Forgive us for the places in our lives that are false or frozen. Christ have mercy.
All	Christ have mercy.

There may be silence or free prayer on this theme.

Reader	In Ninian was a radiant face and a fruitful frame; Forgive us for the places in our lives which are tarnished and unfruitful. Lord have mercy.
All	Lord have mercy.

There may be silence or free prayer on this theme.

Leader   Lord –
Ninian was the guileless one, take from us all guile.
Ninian was the tireless one, take from us all sloth.
Ninian was the fearless one, take from us all cowardice.
Ninian was the radiant one, take from us all that clouds the soul.

Leader   We pray for modern Ninians who will establish communities of light in slum places; sanctuaries of prayer in unvisited places; and links of faith and love with the continent, our spiritual home.
We pray for all people whose longing would lead them to walk this Way, that they may hear about it;
We pray for those who are beginning to walk this Way that they may find joy in it and tell of it for the salvation of many people.

 There may be singing.

A Blessing

Leader   May the countenance of the Father of glory,
The countenance of the Sun of suns,
The countenance of the radiant Spirit
Pour pure white light abundantly upon you
Hour by hour and for ever.

THE LIFE OF NINIAN OF WHITHORN

In AD 398, just twelve years before the last troops of the Roman Empire withdrew their protection of the native British from Anglo-Saxon invaders, Ninian, a Galloway man, who for ten years had trained to become a Christian priest in Rome, was sent back as a bishop to establish a Christian church amongst his people.

The first wave of Christianity in Britain came to the southern part occupied by the Romans, and this had largely fallen away. The Cymric tribes of the west, and of Strathclyde and Galloway, had never fully integrated into the Roman Empire, and they defended their culture against the invading Anglo-Saxons (as well as against the Gaels from Ireland) for much longer than did the people left behind in Roman Britain. Ninian became an apostle of Christ, not only in his own Galloway, but amongst the Picts beyond the river Tay with their pagan druid ways.

On his way home, according to the traditional view, he stayed in Gaul with Bishop Martin of Tours, who had founded large, informal communities of people with a Christ-like lifestyle; these were a model that inspired Ninian for the rest of his life. Communities like those of Martin became the bastions of Christianity throughout the disastrous conflicts and break-up of Roman society.

On his return crowds welcomed Ninian, who brought masons with him to build Britain's first stone church, which he dedicated to Martin. Although Ninian had a following among his own people, he was bitterly opposed by King Tuduvallus, whose power was threatened, albeit by a kingdom not of this world. Ninian entered into spiritual warfare. The king, struck down with a disease that cost him his sight, became penitent and asked Ninian to forgive him. Echoing Jesus' action with the man whose sins he forgave (Mark 2:10), Ninian forgave him, but also laid hands upon him and healed him. From then on the king warmly supported Ninian's evangelisation programme.

Ninian established churches throughout the region, and ordained presbyters. Now spiritual warfare had to be fought in the church. One unmarried church member who was found to be pregnant accused her presbyter of rape; he denied it. How would Ninian handle this? He was given faith to call forth a rare spiritual gift. At a meeting of the whole church, after he laid hands in prayer on all those who had been baptised, the woman brought up her day-old baby and shouted out her accusations against the presbyter. Ninian fixed his eyes on the infant, and commanded it to speak out if the presbyter was its father. The baby stretched out his little fingers towards another man who was the real culprit, and sounds came from his mouth which everyone understood to mean: 'He is my father.'

The Latin Life of Ninian written by Ailred, Abbot of Rievaux in the twelfth century, is effusive, but genuine enough to mention Ninian's struggle with sexual temptation. He resisted this, and grew in strength of character. Ailred writes of a man whose 'repose no crowd disturbed; whose meditation no journey hindered, whose prayer never grew lukewarm through tiredness'.

Ninian built a Community at today's Whithorn. He recruited sons of leading families in the region to a monastic school. This patterned a radical alternative to the immoral and superstitious ways of their world. It became known as 'Candida Casa', which means a 'shining, glistening white house'. The same word was used in the Latin Bible to describe Jesus' robes at His transfiguration. It seems there was a transfiguring atmosphere in this place that became a lighthouse for northern Britain.

Young men developed into disciples through experience of the kingdom of God totally lived. Discipline sometimes had to be exercised. One young man who had committed a serious offence ran away, rather than face his discipline, taking with him Ninian's staff. He took to sea in a boat which began to leak. This brought him to his knees in penitence and prayer. He struck the leaking side of the boat with Ninian's staff, the leak stopped, and he was saved. He returned to Ninian a changed person, imbued with awe at the signs and wonders God can work, and remained a pillar of support to Ninian thereafter.

We are told that all was love, there was nothing of fear in 'this enpurpled radiant one', and that Ninian died full of years, with his powers undiminished. Although this wave of God was replaced by other godless waves, Ninian's work has remained a model and a beacon of hope for succeeding generations, including our own.

Places to visit

The Whithorn Dig, church and museum, and nearby Ninian's Cave; Ninian's Chapel at the Isle of Whithorn (for pilgrims as they came off the boat).

St Aidan

31st August

Leader   ✠ In the name of the sending Father;
In the name of the gentle Son;
In the name of the teaching Spirit;
In Love's name, the Three-in-One.

Leader   God said: My teaching will fall like gentle rain on tender grass. *(Deuteronomy 32:2)*

Lord, whose gentle apostle Aidan befriended everyone he met with Jesus Christ; give us his humble, Spirit-filled zeal, that we may inspire others to learn your ways, and to pass on the torch of faith.

All   All that I am, all that I do, all whom I'll meet today I offer now to you.

 There may be singing.

A Lindisfarne Rhythm of Praise

Leader   Ebb tide, full tide, praise the Lord of land and sea.
All   Barren rocks, darting birds, praise His holy name!

Leader   Poor folk, ruling folk, praise the Lord of land and sea.
All   Pilgrimed sands, sea-shelled strands, praise His holy name!

Leader   Fierce lions, gentle lambs, praise the Lord of land and sea.
All   Noble women, mission priests, praise His holy name!

Leader	Chanting boys, slaves set free, praise the Lord of land and sea.
All	Old and young and all the land, praise His holy name!

 **The Word of God**

Reader	*Psalm 103:1–18.* *This response may be used after verses 5, 10, 14, 18:*
All	Do not forget how kind He is.

 Alleluias may be sung.

Reader	*Isaiah 6:1–8.*

Reader	*The Poem 'The Mantle of Aidan'.*

Oh Aidan, you had the vision of a population
transformed in Christ.
You had the faith to come.
You had the gentleness to win the hearts of king
and commoner.
You ministered in power and patience to the sick
and dying;
You created teamwork.
Your visits to tell people Good News gave your
team a pattern to follow.
You loved the people of the island.
You lived simply and prayed much.
You prepared a mission to the kingdom.
You influenced many to reach others for Christ.
You are Christ for the nation.
You are apostle to this land.
You are in pain that people here are heedless of
your Lord.
You will not rest till they are won.

Leader	Father, put the mantle of Aidan upon us.

Song

'*I the Lord of land and sea*' (*Here I am, Lord*).

Reader   *Matthew 11:25–30.*

This may be followed by silence, teaching, sharing or singing.

 Prayers

Repentance

Leader   Lord, Aidan was humble and loving; forgive us for
being proud;
Lord, have mercy;

All   Lord, have mercy.

Leader   Lord, Aidan was a faithful shepherd; forgive us for
being faithless;
Christ, have mercy;

All   Christ, have mercy.

Leader   Lord, Aidan brought the torch of Christ for all to
see; forgive us for hiding the light;
Lord, have mercy;

All   Lord, have mercy.

Restoration

Reader   Lord, we of this day are children of confusion;
Restore the vision of God to us.
The noise of the city deafens us to the still small
voice;
Restore the hearing of God to us.
The pace of modern living chokes us;
Restore the alertness of God to us.
The pride of modern living imprisons us;
Restore the liberty of God to us.

We pray for the Holy Island of Lindisfarne:
Here be the peace of those who do your will;
Here be the peace of brother serving other;
Here be the peace of holy ones obeying;
Here be the peace of praise by dark and day.

Reaching out

Reader   Set us free, O God, to cross barriers for you,
As you crossed barriers for us.
Spirit of God, make us open to others in listening,
Generous to others in giving,
And sensitive to others in praying,
Through Jesus Christ our Lord.

We pray for the conversion of the English people . . .
We pray for the renewal of the English Church . . .

We pray that you will raise up new communities
of witness.
We pray for members of the Community of Aidan
and Hilda.
We pray for this church . . . *(free prayer)*.

 There may be singing.

Leader   From today and always may we:
Look upon each person we meet with the eyes of
Christ;
Speak to each person we meet with the words of
Christ;
And go wherever we are led with the peace of
Christ.

THE LIFE OF AIDAN FROM 'BEDE'

It was from this island (of Iona) and this community of monks that Aidan was sent after his consecration as bishop to instruct the English kingdom in the faith of Christ. . . . Among the lessons that Aidan had given the clergy about the conduct of their lives there was none more salutary than his own example of abstinence and self-discipline; and his teaching commended itself to everyone, above all because he taught the way of life that he and his followers practised. He neither sought nor cared for the possessions of this world. . . . He travelled everywhere whether in town or in the country, not on horseback but on foot, unless forced to do otherwise by some urgent necessity, so that, as he walked, wherever he caught sight of people, rich or poor, he could at once turn and speak to them. If they were unbelievers he would invite them to accept the mystery of faith and encourage them by his words and actions in the practice of almsgiving and mercy.

His way of life was in great contrast to the slothfulness of our own times, so much so that all who travelled with him, whether monks or lay people, were required to study, that is to occupy themselves in reading the scriptures or learning the Psalms. This was the daily task of Aidan and all his company wherever they went.

If wealthy people did wrong he never kept silent out of deference or fear, but would correct them with a stern rebuke. He never gave money to powerful men of the world, but only food to such as he entertained; and those gifts of money that he received from the rich he preferred to distribute for the use of the poor, or spend in ransoming people unjustly sold into slavery. In fact many of those he had ransomed later became his disciples, and after training and instructing them he ordained them to the priesthood.

The God who judges our hearts revealed by miraculous signs how great was Aidan's worth. He cultivated peace and love, self-discipline and humility. His heart had the mastery over anger and avarice, and was contemptuous of pride and vainglory. He spared no effort in carrying out and teaching the commands of Heaven, and was diligent in his reading and keeping of vigils. He showed the authority befitting a bishop in rebuking the proud and mighty, and was merciful in bringing comfort to the weak and relief and protection to the poor. In brief, as far as we have discovered from those who knew him, he neglected none of the duties that he learned from the writings of the evangelists, apostles and prophets, but strove with all his strength to fulfil them in his life.

Places to visit

Lindisfarne, Bamburgh Church (where he died); Inner Farne Island (where he went on retreat); Iona (where he trained); Innisboffin in Ireland (where his relics are said to have been taken).

Halloween and All Saints

31st October/1st November

Also for use in prayer walks, celebrations, days of spiritual warfare or as a night prayer.

Leader ✠ We call on the Father of lights.
We call on the Champion of fights.
We call on the Strength of Heaven.

Leader Sin has weakened our resolve:
All Invade us once again.

Leader Sin has blunted our stewardship:
All Invade us once again.

Leader Sin has soured our relationships:
All Invade us once again.

Leader Sin has fragmented your beauteous body:
All Invade us once again.

Leader Sin has set us in frozen isolation:
All Invade us once again.

Leader Sin has blighted our cities and soil:
All Invade us once again.

 There may be singing.

Forgiveness

Leader Light-creator, evil and sin cannot for ever make their home where you are welcomed in.
All Forgive us for the places where your light has been shut out.

Leader	Light-giver, fear and fault-finding have no place where your love is invited in.
All	Forgive us for the places where your love has been shut out.
Leader	Light-conductor, loneliness and self-sufficiency have no place where your saints are welcomed in.
All	Forgive us for the places where we have shut them out.
Leader	Compassionate God of heaven's powers:
All	Screen me from people with evil intentions.
Leader	Compassionate God of freedom:
All	Screen me from curses and spells.
Leader	Compassionate God of the saints:
All	Screen me from bad deeds, bad words, bad thoughts.
Leader	Compassionate God of eternity:
All	Screen me from bad influences here in the past.
Leader	You were here before all these evils, You are here now, You will be here at journey's end.
All	Amen.

Some may wish to make the sign of the Cross ✠

All Your Cross be between me and all things greedy.
Your Cross be between me and all things mean.
Your Cross be between me and all things gruesome.
Your Cross be between me and all things coming darkly towards me.

Some may choose to lay hands on the person on their right.

All God be in your thinking.
God be in your sleeping.
God be in your dying.
God bring you into the company of the saints.

The Word of God

Reader   *Hebrews 12:1, 2; 22– 24.*

Therefore, with all this host of witnesses encircling
us, we must strip off every handicap, strip off sin
with its clinging folds, to run our appointed course
with steadfastness, our eyes fixed upon Jesus as
the pioneer and perfection of faith – upon Jesus
who, in order to reach His own appointed joy,
steadily endured the Cross, thinking nothing of its
shame, and is now seated at the right hand of the
throne of God . . . we have come to the city of the
living God, the heavenly Jerusalem, to myriads of
angels, to the joyful gathering of God's first-born
whose names are written in heaven, to the spirits
of good people made perfect.

*There may be praise singing which enthrones Christ
and displaces all that does not bow the knee to Him.
This may be interspersed with arrow prayers, words or
scriptures such as Philippians 2:5–15.*

Leader   God of strength, God of peace;
          God of time, God of eternity;
          God of the saints;
          In you is all strength;
          You are:
All   Stronger than the elements,
          Stronger than the shadows,
          Stronger than the fears,
          Stronger than human wills,
          Stronger than the spirits,
          Stronger than the magic, spells and vile fantasies
          that assail us.

Leader   Where the Spirit of the Lord is, there is freedom.
In the name of the Sender, the Saviour, the Soul-
friend.
In the name of the Sacred Three.
In the name of God's host of saints we declare:

All   Be free of all distress;
Be free of all that destroys;
Be free of all that divides;
Be free of all that derides.

Leader   May the saints be with us:
With John the loved disciple who soars like an
eagle:
All   We claim the victory of the Lord.

Leader   With the Fathers of the desert who were weaned
from selfishness:
All   We claim the victory of the Lord.

Leader   With Ninian of the shining Household of Faith:
All   We claim the victory of the Lord.

Leader   With Illtud, holy and learned sage:
All   We claim the victory of the Lord.

Leader   With David, flame and faith-builder of Wales:
All   We claim the victory of the Lord.

Leader   With Patrick, slave of Christ and apostle of the
Irish:
All   We claim the victory of the Lord.

Leader   With Brigid, mid-wife of faith to the people:
All   We claim the victory of the Lord.

Leader   With Mungo, faithful pilgrim and founder of
communities:
All   We claim the victory of the Lord.

Leader   With Columba, Christ's giant of the Isles:
All   We claim the victory of the Lord.

| Leader | With Aidan, gentle shepherd and apostle of England: |
| *All* | We claim the victory of the Lord. |

| Leader | With Hilda, bright jewel of the church, gatherer of the faithful: |
| *All* | We claim the victory of the Lord. |

| Leader | With Cuthbert, healer and conqueror of the dark places: |
| *All* | We claim the victory of the Lord. |

There may be singing.

St Patrick's Breastplate

Reader   For my shield this day I call
Strong powers of the angels obeying
In the glorious company of the holy and risen ones,
In the prayers of the fathers,
In visions prophetic,
And commands apostolic,
In the annals of witness,
In the innocence of virgins,
In the deeds of steadfast men.

Around me I gather
These forces to save
My soul and my body
From dark powers that assail me;
Against false prophecies,
Against pagan devisings,
Against heretical lying,
And false gods all around me.
Against spells cast by women,
Against knowledge unlawful,
That injures the body,
That injures the spirit.

For my shield this day I call
A mighty power:
The holy Trinity.

All   The Shield of Christ be over you;
The Shield of Michael be over you;
The Shield of Patrick be over you;
The Shield of Aidan be over you.

Blessing

Leader   Yes,
The shielding of God be with us;
The love of God to enfold us;
The peace of God to still us;
The Spirit of God to fill us;
The saints of God to inspire us;
This hour, this night, for ever.

Matthew the Evangelist, from the Book of Kells

St Hilda

17th November

Leader   ✝ In the name of the Father who fosters;
In the name of the Son who frees;
In the name of the Spirit who freshens;
In the name of the Sacred Three.

Leader   Wisdom lights up the land:
All   She calls us to walk in her ways.

Leader   Wisdom has built a house:
All   She calls us to learn her ways.

Leader   Wisdom is more precious than rubies:
All   We desire her above all things.

All   *The following or another song.*

Christ as a light, illumine and guide me,
Christ as a shield, o'ershadow me.

Christ under me, Christ over me,
Christ beside me, on my left and my right.

This day be within and without me,
Lowly and meek yet all-powerful.

Be in the heart of each to whom I speak,
In the mouth of each who speaks to me.

This day be within and without me,
Lowly and meek yet all-powerful.

Christ as a light, Christ as a shield,
Christ beside me, on my left, on my right.

The Word of God

Reader   *Psalm 34:1–14.*

         This response may be used after verses 3, 7, 10, 14:

All   The Lord is near to those who are discouraged.

Confession

Leader   Hilda was constant in faith throughout her life.
All   Forgive us, Lord, for the times we have been faithless.

Leader   Hilda offered guidance to high and low alike.
All   Forgive us, Lord, for prejudice towards others.

Leader   Hilda fostered excellence in all that was done.
All   Forgive us, Lord, for being content with the second rate.

Leader   May holy Jesus pardon us for these sins, free us from these evils, and empower us into new ways.

Leader   O God our vision, in our mother's womb you formed us for your glory. As your servant Hilda shone like a jewel in the church, may we now delight to claim her gifts of judgment and inspiration reflected in the women and men of this age.

The Word of God

Reader   *Proverbs 8:1–19.*

         A time of reflection.

Reader   *Philippians 4:2–9.*

         In a Communion Service the Gospel of Luke 15:1–10 may be read.

Leader   *Teaching or reading from The Life of Hilda (below).*

         There may be Creative Activities or singing.

Creative Activities

Use the Lament and the Rekindling and Blessing from 'A Whitby Act of Healing' (see the Healing the Land service, page 128) and one of the Creative Activities suggested there. The Lament should precede the following prayers, and the Rekindling and Blessing should follow them.

Prayers

Leader   Blessed are you, God of the planet earth.
You have set our world like a radiant jewel in the heavens,
And filled it with activity, beauty, suffering, struggle and hope.

Blessed are you, God of this land;
In all the peoples who live here,
In all the lessons we have learned,
In all that remains for us to do.

Blessed are you because you need us,
Because you make us worthwhile,
Because you give us people to love and work to do,
For your universe, your world, and for ourselves.

Lord, help us to trade with the gifts you have given us.
Bend our minds to holy learning that we may escape the fretting moth of littleness of mind that would wear out our souls.
Brace our wills to actions that they may not be the spoils of weak desires.
Train our hearts and lips to song which gives courage to the soul.
Being buffeted by trials, may we learn to laugh,
Being reproved, may we give thanks,
And having failed, may we determine to succeed.

There may be free prayer and singing.

Blessing

Leader   May wisdom, truth and fruitfulness abound in
your life;
May you always rejoice in the goodness of your
Maker.
Go in peace with all people to serve Christ in one
another.

All   In the name of the Lord. Amen.

THE LIFE OF HILDA OF WHITBY

Hilda was born in exile from her parents' native Northumbria, but returned there in AD 617. While still young she and her uncle Edwin, Northumbria's first Christian king, were baptised by Paulinus, a missionary sent from Rome. It was the Celtic missionaries, however, who shaped her and with whom she worked closely all her life.

Bede tells us that Hilda lived the first thirty-three years of her life, amongst family and friends, 'very nobly'. Then she made her vows, left them and devoted herself to God in East Anglia, whose king had married her sister. It is believed she also spent some time at Chelles monastery, in Brittany. Soon, however, her great friend Aidan, Bishop of Northumbria, called her back to develop work in his diocese.

After a year learning to live in community with some friends in the Wear, Hilda was made Abbess of the fledgling monastery at Hartlepool by Aidan. Nine years later, when Northumbria's Christian king Oswy had made his kingdom secure, he gave Hilda land to establish a new monastery at what is now Whitby. Here she was able to draw out the creative and spiritual gifts of people, and to establish an ordered framework within which they could flourish.

This institution bore such fruit that it became a double monastery for both men and women. Its fame, together with Hilda's human insight and sense of God's strategy, caused her to be sought out by political and religious leaders. She showed the same quality of care for everybody, however poor or uneducated. It was Hilda who brought the uneducated cowman Caedmon into the monastery, whose songs were to bring the good news of Christ to so many. Her interest in people, her skill in spiritual direction, her fairness, and her refusal to appease arrogant church bureaucrats like Bishop Wilfred, won the affection of the people, and she became known as 'Mother' far beyond the boundaries of Northumbria.

In the monasteries, she inspired devotion to their Rule, to study, and to scripting of the Bible. Her monasteries sent out a stream of notable evangelists and bishops, one of whom, Wilfred, did much to undermine the Celtic simplicities and to impose Roman regulations upon the church. Hilda offered Whitby as a venue for a council to try and resolve the differences between the Celtic and the Roman adherents. It was at this council, in 664, that the Roman regulations were imposed, and some of the disillusioned Lindisfarne monks decided to return to Ireland.

During the last six years of her life Hilda suffered from fever. Bede tells us that 'during all this while she never failed either to return thanks to her Maker, or publicly and privately to instruct the flock committed to her charge'.

Places to visit

Whitby: remains of medieval abbey on the original site; Whitby parish church opposite. Hackness parish church, near Scarborough, which has stone crosses made by Hilda's nuns.

An Everyday Prayer Guide
Through the Celtic Year

This will help you to weave together personal, household or corporate prayer according to the season.

Use Morning Worship for the day of the week, except for short periods that introduce a new season as explained in this Guide. Use Evening Worship for the day of the week, but feel free to replace it with Prayer Around the Cross on Fridays or with the Vigil of Fire on Saturdays. Choose whichever Midday or Night Prayer attracts you, except for suggestions that follow for seasonal use of Night Prayer.

Twenty-Four-Hour Prayers of the Heart

These may be continually repeated with the lips or just with the heart at any moment of day or night. These may be said for oneself or on behalf of a particular person or situation you are interceding for that day.

31st December and 1st January

Use the New Year Service on page 94.

1st–30th January

Use this as your twenty-four-hour prayer of the heart:

Jesus Christ is the Light of the world:
A light no darkness can quench.

Use the following before morning worship and before meals.

In darkness light a candle and say:

Leader Jesus Christ is the Light of the world:
All A light no darkness can quench.

Leader In the beginning was the Word, and the Word was with God, and the Word was God. He was with God in the beginning. Through Him all things were made; without Him nothing was made that has been made. In Him was life, and that life was the light of all people. The light shines in the darkness, but the darkness has not overcome it. *(John 1:1–5)*

Leader Light has come into the world:
All A light no darkness can quench.

Leader The light exposes the deeds of evil:
All A light no darkness can quench.

Leader The light reveals to us the way we should go:
All A light no darkness can quench.

Leader The light shines that we might live by its goodness:
All A light no darkness can quench.

Leader Jesus Christ is the Light of the world:
All A light no darkness can quench.

Leader Christ, as a light,
Illumine and guide me!
Christ as a shield, o'ershadow and cover me.
Christ under me, Christ over me.
Christ beside me, on left and on right,
Christ behind me, Christ before me,
Christ this day within, without me.
Christ as a light,
Illumine and guide me.
The light of Christ has come into the world,
All A light no darkness can quench.

16th January

Instead of the above use Worship for St Fursey's Day on page 145. Use a prayer from this at midday, evening and night, and before a meal.

1st February

Use Worship for St Brigid's Day on page 151 and include a prayer from this at midday, and evening prayer. Use Brigid Night Prayer all week.

1st February to Ash Wednesday

Before a meal say this prayer which is sometimes attributed to Brigid:

I would prepare a feast and be host to the great High King, with all the company of heaven.
The nourishment of pure love be in my house, and the roots of repentance.
May we have baskets of love to give, with cups of mercy for everybody.
Sweet Jesus, be here with us, with all the company of heaven.
May this meal be full of cheerfulness, for this is a feast of the great High King, who is our host for all eternity.

11th February – Caedmon

Use this poem during worship and before a meal:

The first of English poets he
Who nurtured by the Whitby sea
A poor and simple cowherd seemed.
Yet here the gold of poetry gleamed
Though hidden deep within his soul.
For from the company he stole
Fearful to be found afraid
When they their entertainment made.

The very least among the throng
With little speech nor any song.

Then in the stillness of one night
His soul was filled with heavenly light:
A vision of the world being made
Of God's creation all displayed.
As in the stable stall he lay
Dreaming he heard an angel pray,
And speak to him of God's great world
And how its majesty unfurled.
Then day by day to his inspired mind
That had seemed deaf and dumb and blind
There came sweet words so bright and clear.
Then Mother Hilda came to hear
And stayed with all her Abbey folk
While Caedmon, poet of Whitby, spoke.
No longer now to steal away
When came his turn the harp to play,
For in his Saxon mother tongue
Were all his splendid verses sung,
And improvised with great delight
On many a stormy winter's night.
When firelight filled the raftered hall
In far-off ancient Streonshalh.
Then fold would learn the poems by heart
Or memorise a favourite part,
Making them one with Christian praise
In those remote, unlettered days.
And Caedmon's fame was spread abroad
As one who praised in song the Lord.

Ash Wednesday to Good Friday

*Most days you may wish to use Morning Worship for
Fridays and the Passion Season (page 25ff.), and
include a prayer from this in Midday, Evening and
Night Worship.*

Use this as your twenty-four-hour prayer of the heart:

Lord Jesus Christ, have mercy on me, a sinner.

Use this before a meal:

In your mercy, you gave manna to your hungry
people in the desert.
In your mercy you provide for our needs.
Bless this food, and if there is any hungry or
thirsty soul walking along the road,
Send them into us that we can share the food with
them,
Just as you share your gifts with us.

1st March – St David
2nd March – St Chad
17th March – St Patrick
20th March – St Cuthbert

On these days, instead of using the above or Easter
Worship, use the Worship for each saint's day in the
morning, and use a prayer from this at Midday,
Evening and Night Worship, and before a meal.

Good Friday

Use Friday Evening Prayer Around the Cross on
page 49.

Easter Eve

Use the Easter Eve Vigil on page 97.

Daily from Easter to Ascension

Most days you may wish to use Morning Worship for
Sundays and Easter (page 3ff.), and include a prayer
from this in Midday, and Evening Worship, and use
Resurrection Night Prayer.

Use as your twenty-four-hour prayer of the heart:
Christ is risen! Alleluia!

Before a meal, light a candle and say the following, until Pentecost:
Christ is risen! Alleluia!
We give thanks for the goodness of this earth, this food and this fellowship.
Risen Christ of the miraculous catching of fish, and the perfect lakeside meal, we give you thanks for your presence with us as we eat this meal.

From Ascension to Pentecost

Use the Worship for Ascension on page 109 in the morning, and include a prayer from this at Midday, Evening and Night Prayer.

Those who wish to dedicate this period as Nine Days of Prayer should use the first five days to pray throughout the day for that day's gift of the Spirit; use the whole prayer on the following four days. This can also be used before worship and before a meal (using the response for 'All').

Day 1   Come, O Spirit of Love, that goes to any lengths, that breaks through a lifetime's crippling habits, that wells up from the depths,

All   Come, O Spirit of Love.

Day 2   Come, O Spirit of Purity, that burns away lust and wastefulness of time,

All   Come, O Spirit of Purity.

Day 3   Come, O Spirit of Wisdom, that teaches us to see into the nature of things, to know and to do what is right,

All   Come, O Spirit of Wisdom.

| Day 4 | Come, O Spirit of Joy, that brings a song into haggard lives, a serenity into our roots and a sparkle into our eyes, |
| *All* | Come, O Spirit of Joy. |

| Day 5 | Come, O Spirit of Power, that snaps the chains of fear and casts out the demons of hell and hopelessness, |
| *All* | Come, O Spirit of Power. |

The Spirit of Love, of Purity, of Wisdom, of Joy and of Power is coming.

All Even so, come Lord Jesus.

The ties that bound our Saviour to one place are finally gone. Alleluia! Holy Spirit,

Come to us with wisdom.
Come to us with understanding.
Come to us with patience.
Come to us with truth.
Come to us with purity.
Come to us with reverence
Glory to Jesus. Glory to the Father.
Glory to you O ever boundless Spirit.

From Pentecost for seven days

Use the Worship for Pentecost on page 113, and include the following prayer in Midday, Evening and Night Prayer. Use the Pentecost Night Prayer.

| Leader | Spirit of God,
Amongst the wheels of industry: |
| *All* | Renew the face of the earth. |

| Leader | Amongst the computers of commerce: |
| *All* | Renew the face of the earth. |

| Leader | Amongst the crime-infested neighbourhoods: |
| *All* | Renew the face of the earth. |

| Leader | Amongst the tired and broken families: |
| *All* | Renew the face of the earth. |

Leader	Amongst the lonely and the sick:
All	Renew the face of the earth.
Leader	Amongst the drugged and disillusioned:
All	Renew the face of the earth.

Use as your twenty-four-hour prayer of the heart:

Spirit of God, renew the face of the earth.

Use this prayer before a meal:

Holy Spirit of God, you are the source of all that
lives,
Of all that grows,
Of all that provides us with food.
May we know your presence with us as we share
this meal.

Trinity Sunday is one week after Pentecost.

Trinity Sunday for seven days

*Use the Worship for Mondays and the Trinity season
(page 8ff.), and include a prayer from this in Midday,
Evening and Night Worship.*

Use this as your twenty-four-hour prayer of the heart:

Holy and Friendly Three, pour graciously and
generously upon me hour by hour.

Use the same prayer before a meal as for Pentecost.

16th May – St Brendan

*Use the Worship for St Brendan's Day on page 180 and
include a prayer from it at worship throughout the day,
before a meal, and as your prayer of the heart. You
may repeat this for several days.*

4th June – Petroc

Use the Worship for St Samson on page 193, and use a prayer from this, including Petroc's name, throughout the day.

9th June – St Columba

Use the Worship for St Columba's Day on page 186 for Morning Worship, and adapt it for Midday, Evening and Night Worship.

21st June and summer solstice period

Use some or all of the Summer Earth Blessing on page 118, and include prayers from this in Morning, Midday, Evening or Night Worship, and before a meal.

Use this daily as your twenty-four-hour prayer of the heart:

Lord of the solstice, Provider of all,
Take my heart, take my all.

At home, make a cross of flowers and place it in the window for the solstice.

Say this prayer before a meal:

Lord of the solstice, Provider of all,
We give you thanks for the food that earth
brought forth,
For the food that has been stored,
And for the food that we now share.
In the sharing may your light shine forth.

28th June – Irenaeus

Use the Irenaeus Midday Prayer (page 36ff.) and include a prayer from this in the worship throughout the day.

28th July – St Samson

Use the worship on page 193 and include a prayer from this at each act of worship and before a meal.

31st July – Glastonbury Saints

Use the worship for this day on page 200 and include a prayer from this at each other act of worship, and before a meal.

August

Use the Worship for Saturdays and Creation or for St Columba's Day whenever it seems appropriate during August, except for the Saints' Days.

Use this as your twenty-four-hour heart prayer:

Lord, you are my island, in your bosom I rest.

Use this or another prayer before a meal:

Give us O God of the nourishing meal,
Well-being to the body, the frame of the soul.
Give us O God of the honey-sweet milk,
The sap and the savour of the fragrant farms.

5th August – St Oswald
26th August – St Ninian
31st August – St Aidan

Use the worship for these days (pages 204–220) on the eve of each Saint's Day as well as on the day. Include prayers at each act of worship and before a meal.

September

As appropriate to your situation use Worship for Harvests on page 124 and Worship for Creation and Saturday on page 29 from time to time.

Continue the August heart prayer and prayer before a meal.

29th September to 30th October
Use the Worship for Tuesdays and Michaelmas (page 13ff.) frequently in the morning, and include a prayer from this in Midday and Evening Prayer. Use the Michaelmas Night Prayer.

Use this as your twenty-four-hour heart prayer:

Faith in the Three, trust in the One, making all through love.

For use before a meal:

May angels be with us while we eat,
And may we welcome to this table anyone in need,
For they may be another angel to bless us.

26th October – Cedd
Use the Worship for St Aidan on page 217 and use the prayer in this, including Cedd's name in it, in the worship throughout the day.

31st October/1st November
Use the Worship for Halloween and All Saints on page 223; include prayers from this throughout the day, and use parts of this for Night Prayer.

All Saints to Advent
As an introduction to worship throughout the day, before a meal, and as the twenty-four-hour heart prayer:

For my shield this day I call
Strong powers of angels obeying;
The glorious company of the holy and risen one,
The light of the King of heaven and earth.

6th November – Illtud

Use the Worship for St David on page 158, and use the prayer in this, including Illtud's name in it, throughout the day.

11th November – Martin of Tours

Use this prayer throughout the day:

Lord, we thank you for Martin, soldier, servant and soul-winner.
Inspired by his example we pray:
Give to us discipline for Christ;
Give to us the heart of stillness that desires to enjoy you alone;
Give to us compassion towards others;
Give to us gifts of organisation;
Give to us an eye for building others up.

Advent

Usually use the Morning Worship for Wednesday and Advent (page 17ff.).

Use the following before worship at other times, as your twenty-four-hour heart prayer, and before meals:

Calm us to wait for the gift of Christ;
Cleanse us to prepare the way for Christ;
Teach us to contemplate the wonder of Christ;
Teach us to know the presence of Christ;
Anoint us to bear the life of Christ.

In the house create an Advent wreath with four white candles, and a coloured candle in the middle.

Advent to 6th January

Use the following weekly at a household meal: one candle the first week etc. From Christmas light all five candles.

Different persons light the four Advent candles with these words:

1. This is the candle of longing; may our hopes for all that is good come to pass *(each person may say or think of some good thing they long for).*
2. This is the candle of expecting; may all that prophets foretold come to pass *(each person may say or think of a promise in the Bible of something God will do).*
3. This is the candle of preparing; may all that gets in the way of God be cleared from our lives *(each person may say or think of something they wish to be rid of).*
4. This is the candle of bearing; as Mary let Jesus be born in her, may we let his presence be born amongst us *(in silence each person invites Jesus to be born anew in their hearts).*
5. *Now another person lights the big candle in the middle with these words:*
This is the candle of Christ, the Light of the world, who has come amongst us today.

Christmas Eve

Make this a day of spiritual as well as of practical preparation. Use the Christmas Eve Vigil on page 90.

Christmas Eve to 6th January

Use the Morning Worship for Thursday and the Incarnation (page 21), and include a prayer from this in the worship at other times, or the following prayer:

Christ is the Gift to us who live here.
Son of the Dawn, Son of the planet,
Son of the sky, Sun of the earth,
Son of the elements, Sun of the heavens,
Son of Mary of the mind of God,
Son of God, first-born of all creation
Is now among us. Alleluia!

Use this as your twenty-four-hour prayer of the heart:

O come let us adore him, Christ the Lord.

Use this as a prayer before a meal:

Hail King, blessed are you. Let there be joy!
Bless the King, without beginning, without ending;
Who is everlasting, let there be joy.
Bless this meal and all it contains;
Deliver this house from all that stains;
Be health to us all and cure our pains.

Notes

1   The Community of Aidan and Hilda is a network of Christians and churches who follow a common way of life that draws inspiration from the Celtic saints. Head office: Red Hill Farm, Snitterfield, Stratford-Upon-Avon, CV37 0PQ.

2   In a foreword to *Celebrating Common Prayer* (Mowbray, 1992).

3   In *The Second Letter to the People of God*, Taizé, written at Calcutta-Chittagong 1976.

4   Lectionaries for daily use include:
The Ecumenical Daily Office (Joint Liturgical Group/ SPCK);
The Church of England *Alternative Service Book* (Mowbray);
The Roman Catholic Divine Office (Collins);
Celebrating Common Prayer (Mowbray);
Encounter with God Daily Notes, Scripture Union, 207/209 Queensway, Bletchley, Milton Keynes MK2 2EB.
The Bible in a Year: Every Day with Jesus;
Daily readings for Midday in Taize Newsletter's Johannine Hour.

5   In a foreword to *Celebrating Common Prayer* (Mowbray, 1992).

6   *Baptism, Eucharist and Ministry*, a Report of the World Council of Churches.

7   *The Eucharist*, Alexander Schmemann, St Vladimir's Seminary Press, New York 1988.

8   A Celtic symbol of the Holy Spirit.

Sources and Acknowledgments

I would like to thank Frances Clarke of Bowthorpe for typing the second drafts, and church leaders and members of the Community of Aidan and Hilda for their feedback after trial use.

Quotations from the Bible are based on *The Good News Bible* (Harper Collins), the *New International Version* (Hodder and Stoughton) or are the author's own translation.

Morning Worship for Sunday and the Easter Season
'Spring with her colour . . .' from a poem by Peter Howard in *Peter Howard, Life and Letters* by Anne Wolrige Gordon, with permission of the Oxford Group.
'Jesus said: . . .' Mark Slater.

Morning Worship for Monday and the Trinity Season
'The Three who are over my head . . .' *Carmina Gadelica*.
'For my shield this day . . .' Echoes Patrick's Breastplate, traditional.

Morning Worship for Tuesday and the Michaelmas Season
'The shield of Christ . . .' *Carmina Gadelica* (adapted).

Morning Worship for Wednesday and the Advent Season
'Wisdom, Breath of the most High . . .' Echoes the Advent Great O's, traditional.

Morning Worship for Thursday and the Incarnation Season
'That was the time of the Great Nativity . . . and the soles of his feet . . .' *Carmina Gadelica*, adapted.

Morning Worship for Saturday and the Creation Season
'For earth and sea . . .' Echoes a prayer of George MacLeod in *The Whole Earth Shall Cry Glory*, with permission from Wild Goose Publications.
'I believe . . .' *Carmina Gadelica*.

Midday Prayer
'Lead me from . . .' The International Peace Prayer, adapted.
'Bless us now Lord . . .' from Taizé, adapted.

Evening Worship for Sunday to Wednesday
'Light of the world . . .' Revd Paul Gibson, with permission
Intercessions for each day. Much of this material is inspired by the pattern used by Marjorie Milne, of Glastonbury, whose story has been told in *Glastonbury Journey* by Brian Frost (Becket Publications, 1986); some of this in turn is drawn from more ancient Christian tradition.

Evening Worship for Thursday to Saturday
'May the Light of lights . . .' *Carmina Gadelica.*
'You are my island . . .' Attributed to Columba.
'Lighten our darkness' *Book of Common Prayer*, adapted.

Friday Evening Prayer Around the Cross
'O my people . . .' Traditional.
'On you was crucified' *Carmina Gadelica.*
'May the Cross of Christ' From verses attributed to Mugron, Abbot of Iona from 965.

Saturday Evening Vigil of Fire
'O thou who camest . . .' Charles Wesley.
'King of the sun . . .' In Robert Van der Weyer, *Celtic Fire,* unattributed.
'Kindle in our hearts . . .' Attributed to Columba.

Night Prayer General Theme
'I place my soul and body . . .' Adapted from *Carmina Gadelica.*
'O Christ . . .' From Robert Van de Weyer, *Celtic Fire,* unattributed.
'I lie down this night with God . . .' *Carmina Gadelica.*

Night Prayer Resurrection Theme
'Risen Christ, watch over this night . . .' *A New Zealand Prayer Book,* with permission of the Church of the Province of New Zealand (Collins).

Night Prayer Michaelmas Theme
'O angel guardian . . .' and 'May the seven angels . . .' *Carmina Gadelica.*

A Celtic Holy Communion
'The Offering' inspired by David Adam of Lindisfarne.
'The Thanksgiving' reflects the Stowe Missal, in F. E. Warren, *The Liturgy and Ritual of the Celtic Church* (Boydell).

Winter Solstice
'Creator of the Universe . . .' *A New Zealand Prayer Book*, with permission of the Church of the Province of New Zealand (Collins).
'Glow to him . . .' Echoes a prayer from the *Carmina Gadelica*.

An Alternative Christmas
'Jesu you are . . . never forsake us' Echoes a prayer in the *Carmina Gadelica*.
'Infant Jesus . . .' Echoes the Litany of the Infant Jesus of Prague.
'Homemaker God' Revd Michael Mitton.

New Year
'I said to the man . . .' 'The Desert' by M. Louise Haskins.
'Be a smooth way before me . . .' Attributed to Columba.
'God be with you at every leap . . .' *Carmina Gadelica*.

Easter Eve Vigil
'O King of the Friday . . .' Ancient Irish.
'Christ harrows hell . . .' Brother Ramon SSF.

Easter Sunrise Service
'Rejoice, heavenly powers! . . .' Traditional.
'Christ our Passover' Traditional.

Pentecost
'Holy Spirit of greatest power . . .' Echoes the prayer of the poet Mael Isu tenth century (in *God to Enfold: Praying in the Celtic Tradition*, Mary Calvert, Grail Publications).

Summer Earth Blessing
'Lord bless this soil . . .' Echoes a North American Indian blessing.
'Bless to us, O God' *Carmina Gadelica*.

Harvests
'An Iona Benedicite' E. D. Sedding.
'Bless O God . . . You who put beam . . . Bless to us O God . . .' *Carmina Gadelica*.

Healing the Land
'The sun concealed its proper light . . .' Blathmac, eighth-century Irish in *A Golden Treasury of Irish Poetry* AD 600–1200 (Macmillan, 1967).
'We swear by peace and love . . .' Ancient Celtic (In *The Little Book of Celtic Blessings*, Caitlin Matthews, Element).

Prayer Walks
'O King of the Tree of Life' In Robert Van der Weyer, *Celtic Fire*, DLT 1990, unattributed.

St Fursey
'A Vision . . .' During a vision Fursey was heard to say 'The God of gods shall be seen in Zion' and 'The saints shall advance from one virtue to another'.
'Penitence . . .' This reflects Fursey's vision of the four fires of God's judgment.
'Good and gracious God . . .' Revd Adrian Leighton.

St Brigid
'You who put beam . . . Mary's Son, my Friend . . .' Echoes of prayers in *Carmina Gadelica*.

St David
'Hail, glorious Lord! . . .' Adapted from Llyfr Du Caerfyrddin in Oliver Davies and Fiona Bowie, *Celtic Christian Spirituality: An Anthology of Medieval and Modern Sources* (SPCK).
Gerald Cambrensis, *Description of Wales* (Penguin).
Gwenallt's portrayal of David from Patrick Thomas, *Candle in the Darkness* (Gomer Press, Wales).

St Chad
'Saviour and Friend . . .' Anonymous, collected by Alistair Maclean in *Hebridean Altars*.
'The Lord Christ go with you . . .' Northumbria Community.

St Patrick
'I arise today . . .' Echoes the traditional St Patrick's Breastplate.
'Christ be beside me . . .' J. Quinn.
'There is no other God . . .' Attributed to St Patrick.

St Brendan
'Father be with us on every road . . . The God of life . . .' *Carmina Gadelica*, adapted.
'Jesus who stopped the wind . . .' Revd Alistair Mackichan.

St Columba
'Kindle in us . . .' Attributed to Columba, adapted.
'Those who seek the Lord . . .' These are the last words Columba inscribed.
'Lord, you are my island . . .' Echoes a prayer of Columba.
'Dearest Lord . . .' After a poem attributed by some to Columba.

Glastonbury Saints

'Gildas the Wise . . . King Lucius the Glorious . . .' These lines are from a liturgy by Fr John Ives of the British Orthodox Church within the Coptic Patriarchate.

'May these islands receive afresh . . .' Gildas.

St Oswald

'High King of heaven . . .' Echoes the prayer of St Oswald's Church, Durham.

St Ninian

'Almighty God, Creator . . .' Echoes a prayer of George MacLeod in *The Whole Earth Shall Cry Glory* (Wild Goose Publications).
'What is best in this world? . . .' Attributed to Ninian, in Robert Van der Weyer, *Celtic Fire* (DLT).

St Aidan

'Lord, we of this day . . .' Echoes a prayer of George MacLeod in *The Whole Earth Shall Cry Glory* (Wild Goose Publications).
'Here be the peace . . .' Traditional, adapted.
'Set us free, O God . . .' Brother Bernard SSF.
The Life of Aidan from *The Illustrated Bede* translated by John Marsden, with permission.

St Hilda

'Christ as a light . . .' St Patrick, arranged by John Michael Talbot.
'O God our vision . . .' St Hilda Community, adapted.
'Trade with the gifts . . .' Echoes a Homily of St Hilda, available from Whitby Parish Church, unattributed.

Everyday Prayer Guide
11 February Caedmon

'The first of English poets he . . .' Tom Stamp in *Brother Caedmon*, published by Caedmon of Whitby, 1982.

Illustrations

Pages 96 and 222, copyright Marygate House Trust, Holy Island.
Pages 28, 143, by Lindsay Attwood, copyright Michael Mitton.
Page 65, copyright Pam Pott of Earthshire, 58 Geoffrey Road, Brockley, London SE14 1NZ.